Soft Bodies in a Hard World

Soft Bodies in a Hard World

Spirituality for the Vulnerable

Charles Davis

Anglican Book Centre
Toronto, Canada

1987
Anglican Book Centre
600 Jarvis Street
Toronto, Ontario
Canada M4Y 2J6

Typesetting by Jay Tee Graphics Ltd.

Canadian Cataloguing in Publication Data

Davis, Charles, 1923-
  Soft bodies in a hard world

ISBN 0-919891-80-2

1. Christian life — 1960- . 2. Faith.
3. Christian life — Biblical teaching. I. Title.

BV4501.2.D38 1987   248.4   C88-093131-0

For my wife Florence

We seek detachment from the body, wanting to convince ourselves that the real "I" is not this quaking mass of tissue with all its repulsive possibilities for pain and corruption. It is little wonder that we expect religions, philosophies, and other forms of wisdom to show us above all else a way of deliverance from suffering, from the plight of being a soft body in a world of hard reality.

Alan W. Watts, *Nature, Man and Woman*

Contents

Subversive Sayings

I was once asked in a discussion group to choose my favourite sayings of Jesus and comment upon them, giving the reasons for my choice. When I tried to do this, I immediately saw that the answer depended upon the initial choice of a criterion of selection. For example, if my criterion was the impact of the sayings upon my affectivity, or, to put it less pompously, if I chose the sayings that moved me most quickly and strongly, I should come up with sayings such as: "Father, forgive them; for they know not what they do" (Lk 23:34); or, "Blessed are you poor, for yours is the kingdom of God" (Lk 6:20). My reflection led me to do something different. I wanted to select sayings that in one way or another answer for me the question, Why am I still a Christian? Which are the sayings that define for me what it means to be a Christian, sayings that convey attitudes and values which for me are peculiarly Christian, inasmuch as I personally have not found them, at least in combination, elsewhere? I chose the following sayings.

1 "No one can come to me unless the Father who sent me draws him; and I will raise him up at the last day" (Jn 6:44); to be taken with: "and I, when I am lifted up from the earth, will draw all men to myself" (Jn 12:32).

This pair of sayings define human existence as a field of tension in which one is drawn by God towards God, with Christ as mediator. Human life is not a closed, rounded off, complete value, sufficient to itself. It is essentially an openness to what is beyond it. Through it one is drawn to God as transcendent reality. A human being may be defined as a capacity for the Infinite. As Augustine put it, human freedom is to love the good, to delight in it, to be drawn by it, so that to be fully free is to love the Supreme Good or, in other words, to love God above all things. In a modern context, Teilhard de Chardin insisted that evolution was a drawing from before, not a push from behind. Human life does not have its centre within itself. It is pulled into God to share the life of God, to delight in God.

Because human life at its deepest is a participation in the life of God, it is not destroyed by death. As a field of tension open to the attractive force of God, human life persists beyond the grave and takes on the new conditions imaged as the resurrection of the body. Jesus Christ is the mediator of our sharing in the life of God, both as exemplifying a truly human life lived in God and as the channel of the divine force that makes it possible. But it was not their reference to the resurrection or to the role of Christ that led me to choose these texts.

What I had chiefly in mind was the fundamental difference it made to define human life as an openness to God, a capacity for the Infinite. It makes any merely human scale of values relative. Indeed, it subverts those values as commonly understood. The rich, the successful, the powerful in human terms do not rank above the poor, the failures, the weak. More often than not, they rank below, because the openness of human life is more readily recognized by the weak and foolish in the world's eyes than by the wise and strong of this world. It means that human life is essentially a gift from above. It means we cannot rely on our own abilities for the really important things. And when the situation seems hopeless humanly speaking, its resolution may be at hand, if a few just men and women trust in God.

I will put it this way. Because of the years I have spent trying to live out Christian values, I should find it easier to be a nihilist than a secular humanist. Nihilists deny all truth and all values whether divine or human, but, in doing so, they at least recognize the inadequacy of human resources to meet the exigencies of human existence. Secular humanists suppose that human reason, human values, human culture, human endeavour will bring social peace, cultural vitality, rational progress, and a real though limited happiness. They have the greater delusion. Human life is either diabolically evil or supernaturally good. It cannot be enclosed within the merely human.

2 "For whoever would save his life will lose it, and whoever loses his life for my sake will find it" (Mt 16:25).

This saying expresses the basic paradox that distinguishes Christian living from every movement of self-actualization. It is particularly pertinent today when we are surrounded by movements giving us their recipes for physical, mental, and spiritual health and telling us how to succeed in life. Christian belief is that it is through suffering, failure, and death that we attain to life and glory. Human existence for Christians is not, or at least should not be, a search for physical health or a striving for psychic integration or a pursuit of spiritual perfection. That does not mean to say that Christianity demands a glorification of illness or a complacent acceptance of psychic disorder or an indifference to the value of spiritual or contemplative progress. To suppose that would be an inverted form of self-concern. When human wholeness in its various aspects is given to us or made possible, we should rejoice in it with thankfulness as in a gift of God. If we can facilitate its attainment by others, we should do so. Christians have always cared for the sick. Nevertheless, Christian faith does not take its stand upon human wholeness. It is a total risk — the risk of everything — for what is represented by Christ, namely, the transcendent reality of God.

As Christians, we can be called upon to give up everything — bodily health, psychic balance, and progress in contemplative states of consciousness — for the one thing necessary, that is, love of God and fidelity to what we recognize as his call. We are perhaps readier to admit the merely relative value of bodily health than the similarly relative value of the other elements of self-fulfilment. But the Canadian Catholic novelist, Morely Callaghan, showed, I think, a sound instinct in allowing the priest-hero of *Such Is My Beloved* to end his days in a mental home in a state of psychic breakdown. Again, it is a commonplace that Christian contemplatives come out of their contemplative retreat when God's call directs them to devote themselves to the needs of others.

Self-actualization is not a Christian ideal. The self is neither the centre of the universe nor the centre of our own lives. To be Christian is to be decentred, to find our centre of gravity in God and not in ourselves. No doubt the saying tells us that in losing our life we shall find it. But the finding is in a different order; it is not just another version of human self-fulfilment. The resurrection is not the restoration of this life, the reanimation of a corpse, but the entry into a new existence, where God not the self is the centre.

3 "And when evening came, the owner of the vineyard said to his steward, 'Call the labourers and pay them their wages, beginning with the last, up to the first.' And when those hired about the eleventh hour came, each of them received a denarius. Now when the first came, they thought they would receive more; but each of them received a denarius" (Mt 20:8-9). (This is an excerpt from the parable of the labourers in the vineyard, and is intended to stand for the whole parable.)

Although one would have thought that the message of this parable had by now become familiar to Christians, its deeply subversive character is shown by the objections it raises from even good Christians each time it is read. The owner of the vineyard acted unfairly. That is the constant complaint. But human existence at its deepest level is not a matter of rewards proportionate to merit. If we reflect upon our lives, we shall find that at the basis of those achievements we regard as peculiarly our own, as due to some special effort or struggle on our part, there is always a gratuitous factor, something unearned, something unmerited. Human life is essentially a gift, even at the natural level. Our achievements are never fully or basically our own. Hence all social distinctions based upon achievement and reward, upon success and wealth, are at the most of limited, transitory value. How much more is that the case in the realm of grace, where we all need the gift of forgiveness and are freely invited by God into a share in his life!

The acknowledgement that all we are, have, or do is in the last analysis a gift should make us rejoice in the good received by others as though it were our own. It should also make us compassionate with the losses experienced by others. The labourers of the first hour should have rejoiced that the labourers of the eleventh hour received such a generous gift, and had that not happened, they should have been sad that those labourers had to be content with a small wage. That such a demand strikes us as unreal is an indication of how far we are from making the gospel teaching our own.

4 "But Jesus said to him, 'Follow me and leave the dead to bury their own dead'" (Mt 8:2); "Again I tell you, it is easier for a camel to go through the eye of a needle than for a rich man to enter the kingdom of God" (Mt 19:24).

These are shocking statements. They shock and continue to shock, even when familiar by repetition, because they overthrow the scale of values upon which every human society is built. After all, "rich" is not an absolute, but a relative term. It describes those who have made it in any society, whatever may be the absolute amount of wealth. What Jesus is saying is that those who are on top in worldly terms, those who have abundant goods, power, and success in this world, will have the least chance of sharing in the transcendent destiny open to human beings. Indeed, so great is the conflict between making it in this world and entering the kingdom of God, that even the ordinary pieties of life in this world, such as concern to mark the death of our fellow human beings, especially the death of the great, with solemnity, lose their importance and must, if need be, give way. Let the dead bury their dead.

The sayings, I should add, are hyperbolic; in other words, they use exaggeration to make their point. One would miss the transcendence they express if one were to take them literally and try to build a social order upon them. They are not meant to serve as the charter for a new social order. They teach the relative and transitory value of any social order, with its conventions and scale of values. In every social order this world knows, those who are on top of the social ladder may be on the lowest rung of the ladder of the kingdom, if on that ladder at all. To try to make these sayings the basis for an institutional order in this world is to end in a contradiction that destroys the paradox and loses the transcendence. That is what happened with the attempts to institutionalize radical poverty. They resulted in the comparative security and comfort of a religious poverty that knew nothing of the insecurity and privations of the ordinary poor. A radical detachment from the things of this world is called for, not a denial of their necessity or of their value in their own order. Human beings are, however, offered a higher destiny.

5 "Hear and understand: not what goes into the mouth defiles a man, but what comes out of the mouth, this defiles a man" (Mt 15:10–11).

The context of this saying is the disregard by Jesus and his disciples of the laws of purity, requiring that the hands be washed before eating. But the bearing of the saying is much wider. In the light of the general conduct of Jesus and of similar sayings, it is a refusal to regard traditional religious ritual as binding in any absolute fashion. Religion itself, in the sense of religious institutions, religious ritual and practices, religious traditions of all kinds, is relative, changing, dispensable, and not to be made an absolute, which would make it an idolatry. This opens the way to religionless Christianity, not in the sense of a Christianity without customs, ritual, institutions, or traditions, but a Christianity able to change or surrender any of these elements when the ongoing presence of the transcendent in history calls for that.

Unfortunately, Christians have been only too ready to proclaim the desuetude of the Jewish laws of purity, while absolutizing their own institutions and rituals in a far more idolatrous fashion. The saying of Jesus should be interpreted in a self-critical way.

6 "You have heard that it was said, 'You shall love your neighbour and hate your enemy.' But I say to you, Love your enemies and pray for those who persecute you, so that you may be sons of your Father who is in heaven; for he makes his sun rise on the evil and on the good, and sends rain on the just and on the unjust. For if you love those who love

you, what reward have you? Do not even the tax collectors do the same? And if you salute only your brethren, what more are you doing than others? Do not even the Gentiles do the same?'' (Mt 5:43-7).

This is the last in my selection of sayings and one which for me expresses the essential principle of Christian living. It is not simply that we are asked to love others, including our enemies. It is the kind of love we are asked to have or rather allowed to share. The love described in the saying is a creative, not just a responsive love. In other words, it is not a love that simply responds to a goodness already there in those loved; not even a love that simply seeks out the least vestige of goodness, so as to respond to it by nurturing it — the kind of love that finds goodness in the worst of our enemies. No, it is the kind of love that does not presuppose goodness, but creates it. That is why it is a sharing in the love which God has for us his creatures. No goodness in us preceded the love that God has for us; his love created all our goodness.

We are asked to love in the same fashion. If we do, we shall not wait to perceive the spark of goodness in others. We shall go out to meet them, even when we cannot discern anything that renders them lovable, and our love will go out from us as a transforming force. Only thus will we break the cycle of injury and vengeance, only thus will we call a halt to the cumulative effect of hatred responding to hatred. Our love like God's, as a share in God's love, must be utterly gratuitous. It must not demand lovableness as its condition, but anticipate and create lovableness.

Once more we are brought up against the transcendence which Christian faith acknowledges and expresses. That faith subverts all our human values and the worlds we build upon them, but in doing so it takes them up into a higher order in which they are transformed, not destroyed.

Forgiveness

The present un-Christian world does not know the meaning or place of forgiveness. People do not think of themselves as in need of forgiveness to the very depths of their being, nor do they know how to forgive others. We Christians breathe in the surrounding culture, and so we need to make clear to ourselves what we should understand by forgiveness.

Forgiveness does not mean that the offence does not matter. To forgive is not the same as to dismiss or trivialize the wrong done. The Crucifixion is the image of God's forgiveness, and crucifixion is not trivial. The list of what is conventionally regarded as important varies from time to time. People sometimes suppose they are forgiving when in fact they are dismissing a violation no longer considered important. But when the offence is not trivial by their standards, they do not forgive.

Again, forgiveness does not mean wiping the slate clean, forgetting the past, pretending it didn't happen, or beginning again as if nothing had occurred. That kind of repression on the part of either the offender or the offended is not forgiveness. It is neither psychologically nor religiously sound to reject the guilt that arises from an intentionally wrongful action.

Forgiveness is a transformation. It is a process of spiritual healing. Physical healing is never a simple restoration to the state prior to the illness. Sickness followed by healing permanently changes the organism — for the better, if the healing is complete. So, too, with spiritual healing.

There are overlapping phases in the healing process of forgiveness. In the first phase the offender is brought to acknowledge the offence committed. A doctor cannot heal unless the patient acknowledges the illness. To be forgiven people must be led to acknowledge their offences — fully, sincerely, not as a matter of words. There must be a felt need for forgiveness, a longing for a love that will cleanse, transform, recreate the guilty self. This acknowledgement of guilt is then in the second phase pervaded by such a forgiving love. Forgiveness in the forgiver is a creative love, creative inasmuch as it is able to bring about a reversal, in which the offence itself becomes the occasion to move to a new level, a new relationship, a transformed state. Forgiver and forgiven, now reconciled, do not simply resume where they left off, but begin what is new.

To forgive in the sense of offering the person offending a new, deeper relationship requires a creative love of exquisite delicacy. Forgiving may easily become an exercise of power. "I'll forgive you" may spring from a desire to humiliate and dominate. Genuine forgiveness in contrast means taking the other's offence upon oneself, feeling its burden, suffering in and with the offender, condemning the bad, but not denying the good mixed up with the bad in every offence. We can achieve such a positive, discriminating, and creative attitude only if we acknowledge our own need for forgiveness. For us sinful creatures, egocentric and prone to domination, forgiving others can spring only from our own forgiveness. We can be forgivers, only because we ourselves are forgiven and experience our own need to be forgiven and accept forgiveness.

The model for our forgiving is to be found in God. His love, creative and redeeming when confronted with human sin, is the archetype of all forgiveness. Forgiveness indeed may be defined as the response of God to human sin. Our own forgiving is a share in that response. What, then, is God's forgiving?

Humans are deeply sinful. Their sinfulness is, in Augustine's words, "a love of self even to the contempt of God." There is an evil unbalance in human beings, which need not have been so, but which actually pervades human history. This is a refusal to acknowledge God as the centre of reality and of our lives, a refusal to surrender to his love, and, instead, a placing of ourselves as our own centre and a determination to follow our own wills rather that to yield to the promptings of God. God's response to human sin was not, as it might have been, to annihilate us sinners, nor was it to ignore the sin and excuse us poor creatures as not worth bothering about. His response was the more complex one of forgiveness, respecting human dignity but overcoming the power of sin.

Like human forgiveness, divine forgiveness has two phases, which may be distinguished but not separated. The first phase finds expression in the biblical theme of the divine wrath. God's anger is not the avenging rage of a threatened potentate, but stands for all those actions of his that are directed to bringing us to acknowledge our sins. That acknowledgement is a necessity if forgiveness is to be an offer of reconciliation made to human persons in their dignity and freedom. For that reason the divine mercy cannot be separated from the divine wrath. Much pain and chastisement may be required before we acknowledge our guilt. All through, the divine wrath is directed by the divine mercy, but in the second phase of forgiveness, the divine mercy becomes predominant. The second phase is the phase of transforming love. God identifies himself with us sinners, enters into our sinful history and brings about a redemptive process of reversal, in which our sins serve to bring us to a new and deeper relationship with himself. We probably all can recognize how an offence, once forgiven, can be the occasion for a deeper relationship. That kind of reversal is what God achieved in Jesus Christ on the level of human history as a whole. In Jesus God took our sinful humanity upon himself and inaugurated a process of forgiveness capable of transforming human history.

The divine forgiveness in its second phase may be seen as the divine gift *par excellence*, the messianic gift, the very meaning of the kingdom. "Drink of it, all of you; for this is my blood of the covenant, which is poured out for many for the forgiveness of sins" (Mt 26:28). In a sense our whole Christian life, with its experiences, its thoughts, and its institutions, may be brought under the heading of forgiveness.

Matthew, the author of the First Gospel, has been called "the theologian of forgiveness." It is in that gospel we find the emphatic form of a saying on forgiveness. We read:

> Then Peter came up and said to him, "Lord, how often shall my brother sin against me, and I forgive him? As many as seven times?" Jesus said to him "I do not say to you seven times, but seventy times seven." (Mt 18:21-2)

Forgiveness in other words is beyond all calculation.

Immediately preceding the saying on forgiveness is the passage which has served as the legitimation of the Church's discipline of penance and of its claim to forgive sins in the name of Jesus.

"Truly, I say to you whatever you bind on earth shall be bound in heaven, and whatever you loose on earth shall be loosed in heaven" (Mt 18:18). To understand the gospel teaching on forgiveness as a whole, it is helpful to distinguish three dimensions or elements of the process of forgiveness: institutional, intellectual, and mystical; or, to put it in another way, fact, thought, and experience.

To begin with, the institutional. Forgiveness is social, not just personal. It involves the whole community and is, therefore, ecclesial. As a sacred reality made visible, it is sacramental. For both reasons it must be embodied in institutions, ritualized, and regulated. The penitential discipline of the Church has taken various forms at various times. Not unknown in the past and in some churches today is the public denunciation of those who sinned or public acknowledgement of guilt on the part of the sinners themselves. The practice did not always work out happily. The humility and the delicacy required by the forgiving community were not always present. Recall Nathaniel Hawthorne's novel *The Scarlet Letter*. But is the situation today satisfactory? There is no public way of acknowledging guilt, except in the most general terms by the whole community. Hence where a serious offence is publicly known, the perpetrators never go near the Church again. Would not our local communities be more Christian if we were able publicly and lovingly to welcome back repentant ex-prisoners, reformed drunkards and prostitutes, and other known sinners? A ritual reconciliation would enable both sides to do so in the right frame of mind and without embarrassment. I admit that it will not be easy to develop a penitential discipline which would genuinely correspond to our present culture and mentality, but the first step is to feel the lack.

Meanwhile we should be aware that it is one of the functions of the Eucharist to serve as a public expression of both our forgiveness and our forgiving. To quote Matthew again: "So, if you are offering your gift at the altar, and there remember that your brother has something against you, leave your gift there before the altar and go; first to be reconciled to your brother, and then come and offer your gift" (Mt 5:23–4). To join in the celebration of the Eucharist while withholding forgiveness from someone who has offended us is to violate its meaning. The Eucharist is the expression of God's perpetual readiness to forgive. It is the way we seek and implore forgiveness for all our sins. We can make the celebration our own only if we are willing to share in God's forgiving love. If we do come to it in the right disposition, the Eucharist will achieve what it signifies and make our community an embodiment of forgiving love — one that is able to forgive without trivializing the offence or dominating the offender.

The first or institutional dimension of forgiveness gives us forgiveness as a social fact, embodied in the Christian community. The second dimension is that of thought — the intellectual element. Here we meet forgiveness as the focus of our reflection upon the meaning of human existence and human history. What does it mean to worship a crucified Saviour? It implies that human life is very different from what the secular humanists suppose. Human beings are not spontaneously good. They are caught up in a web of selfish desire, in an egocentricity that cuts them off from their true destiny. They come to their true being only through a painful acknowledgement of sin and a surrender to a gratuitous, forgiving, and transforming love. That thought has the power to change not only our individual existence, but also the life of society. Think for a moment of a society in which there was no self-righteousness, but a genuine not hypocritical sense of our common need for forgiveness.

The last dimension of forgiveness is the mystical. Here I refer to the experience of conversion, an experience of being seized by God and brought to a personal recognition of being forgiven. Protestants have frequently exaggerated the dramatic features of conversion and made the whole idea suspect. But the conviction that the recognition of sin and forgiveness brings about a fundamental psychological shift is true, even though that shift need not take place with dramatic suddenness. There is an infinite distance between a human life rooted in egocentric self-sufficiency and one based upon a humble acceptance of God's forgiving love.

However, let us not forget that a fundamental spiritual difference may be carried by what is seemingly minor or unimportant. Take the matter of forgiving others. It is possible to close oneself finally against another person who has hurt our pride or damaged our reputation or confronted us with a weakness we have been trying to hide, but who has not done so in a dramatically serious way, and yet our closure against him or her determines our spiritual destiny. That ''I will not make it up'' is a choice of self against God, a hardening of our heart that is humanly irreversible and will demand a miracle of grace to undo. The great spiritual decisions we make do not always come marked out as such. They may be attached to a minor incident, and a refusal to forgive might well be a beginning of an enduring closure against God.

Weariness in Well-Doing

Towards the end of his Second Letter to the Thessalonians, Paul exhorts them: "Brethren, do not be weary in well-doing" (3:13). A similar exhortation is found in the Letter to the Romans: "Never flag in zeal, be aglow with the Spirit, serve the Lord" (12:11). Although the word itself is not used, these exhortations are warnings against the deadly sin of accidie or, to use the alternative form, acedia.

The traditional list of the seven deadly sins, which older people like myself had to learn in school, is not found as a list in the Bible. For that reason we find a number of alternative versions. One of the variations is to put the sin of accidie instead of the more familiar sloth. Accidie has a wider and deeper meaning than sloth. It is not just laziness. Associated words are "listlessness," "torpor," "discouragement," "weariness," "apathy," "sadness." Basically what is in question is the sin of yielding to a mood of spiritual depression.

There are times when nothing good seems worthwhile or of value. Doing good, living virtuously, serving God, praying, being loving towards our neighbour — all seem pointless. We seem to have lost our taste for everything spiritual. We can hardly bear to go to church. To remain for any time at prayer seems to require an impossible effort. We see those without faith, virtue, or religion prosperous and happy, and we are tempted to say with the people described in Malachi: "It is vain to serve God. What is the good of our keeping his charge or of walking as in mourning before the Lord of hosts? Henceforth we deem the arrogant blessed; evildoers not only prosper but when they put God to the test they escape" (Mal 3:14–5). We become apathetic and without zeal, saying to ourselves, "What is the point?"

Here we must distinguish between accidie as a temptation and accidie as a sin. A listless and discouraged mood is not itself a sin, any more than involuntary lustfull desires are the sin of lust. But temptations have not simply to be resisted when they occur. We must look to see how they arise and endeavour to counter them at their source. Now, accidie has more than one cause. The cause of a weary listlessness in doing good may be bodily or psychological, not directly spiritual. Bodily, psychological, and spiritual factors are inextricably intertwined in our lives. Thomas Aquinas, if I remember correctly, recommended hot baths as a cure for accidie or spiritual depression. I want to dwell here on the spiritual sources of accidie, but that does not imply any denial of bodily and psychological causes and cures. But we must remember that, just as bodily and psychological depression may disguise itself as a spiritual disorder, so, too, what is at root a spiritual malaise, calling for a spiritual remedy, may manifest itself as a bodily or psychological disorder.

Let us now imagine that a mood of discouragement and apathy threatens to overwhelm us. What kind of thoughts will foster it? How can we check the chain of discouraging reflections and overcome our spiritual weariness?

Most of us, looking back on the course of our lives so far, can be brought, when assailed by negative feelings, to see them as wearisome successions of spoilt occasions and lost opportunities. How often have we in our personal lives spoilt a wonderful occasion for enriching an existing relationship or opening a new one? Our selfishness, bad temper, or sheer insensitivity to others have marred what might have been a joyful memory. We can hardly look back upon a holiday or minor celebration without acknowledging that we could have made it much happier. When, more seriously, we look back upon years of parenting or on our life with a spouse now dead, how often does the regret exceed the joy in our recollections! Again, how many opportunities have we lost because of a lack of motivation, a lack of love, an inability to rise to the occasion? Are not our lives meaningless because we have ignored or thrown away what might have given them meaning? Certainly, few of us, if we could live our lives over again would want to leave them just as they have been. Most of us are filled with a profound dissatisfaction with our lives and in our weak moments we are tempted to give up trying and let ourselves drift apathetically, weary of the effort to do good. How shall we counter the temptation to give up?

The first requirement is that we acknowledge that we are finite — acknowledge it, not just in words but in a practical realization of what it means to be limited, fallible creatures. But to talk of acknowledging our finitude is to speak in too grand a manner and to block the acknowledgement we are trying to make. Each one of us needs to recognize his or her limitations. We are, each of us in a particular way, of limited talent, of limited intelligence, of limited energy, of limited virtue, of limited spiritual growth. The pursuit of unlimited economic growth dominates modern society. Unlimited material growth has seemingly become the one aim of social policy. Inadequate as applied to economic activity itself, the pursuit of unlimited growth is disastrous when transferred to other areas of human living. It replaces the reality of human existence with illusory dreams. It destroys the joy in the reality of what we are and have, and fills the empty space with febrile desires. A tranquil and patient acceptance of our limitations as human beings is the first protection against a frequent sinking into listless discouragment.

The second requirement for avoiding a lapse into spiritual weariness is to call a halt to that incessant busyness which is a form of self-inflicted violence. It is violence to allow ourselves to be constantly carried away by a multitude of projects, concerns, and activities. We take on too much. We suppose we can help everyone in everything. We think we are doing fine when we haven't a moment to rest or gather our thoughts. I repeat that such busyness is a form of violence. We destroy joy, we kill the spirit. No wonder we provoke a spiritual sadness and are overcome by weariness, while we drive ourselves forward by frenetic effort. We need to shake off the false conviction that we are not accomplishing anything unless we are caught up in a tumult of activity.

The third line of resistance against accidie or spiritual weariness is engagement in the process of redeeming our sins. We are all sinners, and we sin daily. Sin basically is a failure to love; it is a failure to meet the occasion with the love or spiritual energy it calls for. Demands are made upon us which we can meet only by rising above ourselves, going beyond our own self-interest, beyond our own pleasure, comfort, or advantage. We fail because our openness to others and to reality is too limited to meet the challenge. Whether in small things or in great, we choose ourselves as we are rather than God or Reality, which includes ourselves as we might be if we had greater love. We are constantly sinning, but can we undo sin? Yes, God is our redeemer as well as our creator. But how?

The future gives meaning to the past. That seems strange, but it is true. Suppose, for example, Winston Churchill had died in 1938, before the start of World War II. How differently we should assess his life! As it is, his whole life seems now to have been a preparation for his leadership during the dark days of that War. Again, the first beginnings of Rome as a city were at that time only an unimportant, local event. The future changed their meaning. And so on. We do not as yet know the full meaning of the present events in the Middle East. What will they mean from the standpoint of the future of Islam, Israel, the world? The present meaning of our own individual lives can be radically changed by some event, like marriage, which will give a new meaning to all that has happened to us so far. It is not simply that we do not know the future, but that the future, which is still open, will change the meaning of the present and the past.

The process of redemption is when God's future, becoming our future, transforms our past into a new constellation, a new shape, and gives it a new meaning. In other words, redemption is an openness to the future that allows our past to be transformed into the shape of love. Repentance is not a mere regret for the past, which would be barren and even destructive. It is a transformation which purifies the past by taking it up into a new pattern, as an occasion of growth, a warning, a revelation of fallibility and sinfulness, and so on.

Redemption is a dynamic process of transformation which becomes part of the rhythm of our daily lives. It counteracts accidie or spiritual weariness. Whatever may have been the past, whatever may be the present, God's future lies open before us. God calls us to a share in that future, despite our lowliness as weak and limited creatures, despite our constant lapsing as fallible and sinful humans. The openness of the future is the creative power of God's love. If God's love thus keeps the future open to redeem the past, transform the present, and bring new possibilities to fulfilment, why should we ever lose heart?

Aging into the Resurrection

"If for this life only we have hoped in Christ, we are of all men most to be pitied" (I Cor 115:19). Those are the words of Saint Paul when he reaffirmed the truth of the resurrection of the body to the doubting Corinthians and answerd the difficulties they had raised. His words are a challenge to us today to renew our own belief in the resurrection. We are tempted to avoid the subject, fearing we should find the doctrine incredible and taking refuge in the half-truth that religious faith should not be other-worldly but this-worldly. The remark of Paul makes it clear that Christian hope is illusory if it offers nothing other than this present life.

But let us remove unnecessary difficulties. The resurrection of the body as the truth of our hope for eternal life must not be identified with the reanimation of a corpse. The reanimation of a corpse does provide an image of our overcoming of death by the power of our life in Christ. Just as birth has given us an image for our entry into our new life in Christ, so the raising of a dead body from the tomb is a vivid image of the continuance of our life in Christ beyond death. The image of a reanimated body coming forth from the tomb has given us the very formula, "the resurrection of the body," by which we express our hope for a life that overcomes death. Nevertheless, neither the image nor the words should be allowed to deceive us. What we believe with the help of the image and the words is not that we shall return to this state of existence, but that we shall pass into a new state of existence over which death has no power. For that reason, the raising of Lazarus and the raising of the daughter of Jairus were acted-out images of the resurrection, not instances of the resurrection itself. Lazarus and the daughter of Jairus returned to this existence; our hope is not for a renewal of this life, but for a new and imperishable existence. Again, the function of the empty tomb in the gospel accounts of the resurrection of Jesus is not to identify his resurrection with the reanimation of his corpse, but to offer an almost palpable image of the continued life of Jesus after his crucifixion. In brief, the meaning of the resurrection, both that of Jesus and of ourselves, is that on the other side of death we shall enjoy a new state of existence — everlasting, imperishable, outside the grasp of death.

Yet, that is not to say enough. What distinguishes belief in the resurrection as a particular form of belief in a life beyond death is that it is belief in a bodily after-life. Though it must not be identified with the reanimation of the corpse of the dead person, the resurrection is a transition into a new bodily existence, not an escape from the body. Paul's reply to the difficulties of the Corinthians was not to deny the bodiliness of the risen life, but to point out that there were different kinds of body and that the resurrection body would be a new body. But what is the body?

The body is our personal self when taken in relation to the world and to other people. We do not have bodies; we are our bodies. The body is not an appendage; it is the whole person, but seen in relationship. It is the centre of a network linking the person to the material world, the human world, and other persons.

Belief in the resurrection presupposes a different conception of a human person from that of the Greeks and from that dominant in the West since the philosopher Descartes. For the Greeks the human person was the spiritual soul. Death was the release of the soul from its imprisonment in the body into a purely spiritual existence. It was not simply the corpse after death that was foreign to the true life of the soul; the body itself during life on this earth was alien to our existence as spiritual beings. Descartes made this dualism worse by conceiving the body in a purely mechanical fashion as a mere thing of extension and attributing all the activities of thought and imagination entirely to the soul.

Against all such attempts to deprive human life of its bodiliness, we must, if we are to understand belief in the resurrection of the body, insist that human life is essentially a bodily life. The body is not attached on to us from the outside. It is not a hindrance or a nuisance. The body is nothing less than ourselves — ourselves insofar as we are not isolated monads, but part of systems of relations and interactions wider than ourselves. We are bodies because we are persons with parents, with brothers and sisters and other kindred, because we are related to the animal kingdom, because we are affected by the cycle of vegetation and the change of seasons, because we live in community with other persons, communicating by gesture and language. We are bodies because we are the nodal points of relations and interactions stretching out to the rest of the universe. At death we either cease in our individuality as centres or nodal points — which is what we should most readily think without Christian hope — or we continue as bodies, as individual centres, but in a new fashion.

There is no question of proving the resurrection as a fact. The resurrection is not a matter of verified knowledge, but an object of hope (Rom 8:24). When compared to the certitude of knowledge, hope remains a question, but a question the answer to which is anticipated by the promise contained in faith and the assurance expresed in prayer. Our hope in the resurrection is grounded upon the experience of our relationship of love with God through Christ — an experience which is both our own, personal and individual, and at the same time articulated and confirmed through generations of Christians who have lived out the same relationship with God through Christ. From the time when the apostles and first disciples were converted from their despair at Christ's death to an overwhelming conviction that he was alive and present among them, the Christian community has lived with the faith that the risen Christ is amongst them as the source of new life and with the hope that each will share in the Lord's resurrection.

Reflection, then, upon the resurrection is not an attempt to prove the resurrection to ourselves, let alone to unbelievers. The purpose is simply to uncover some of its intelligibility when considered in the light of faith, and thus to make it a living truth with a practical impact upon the way we live and act.

The body, I have said, is a centre or nodal point. It is our personal self as the intersection point of cycles of activity. These cycles of activity are operative on various levels, so that the lower levels of activity are taken up into the higher, and the higher levels presuppose the lower. Thus, the biological level of activity presupposes and takes up into itself, into its own order and purpose, the lower level of the laws of physics and of chemistry.

Some cycles of activity only gradually emerge; some after a time gradually die away. An example is the cycle of fertility in the woman. It emerges at puberty and ceases with the menopause. The development of intelligence, as Piaget has studied it, is the emergence of cycles of operation, with the higher levels presupposing the lower. The growth of our personality in its interaction and interrelationship with others is again the emergence in sequence of cycles of psychic activities. Further, it is not difficult to conceive the spiritual life of our relationship with God as the gradual emergence of ever higher cycles of activity in a self-transcendence that opens us ever more to the heights and depths of reality.

We can, therefore, think of our bodily selves as dynamic centres, with something of the structure of active spirals. Ever higher cycles of activity are opening up; other cycles are dying away. Death is a critical transition, because it marks the cessation of the whole range of biological cycles of activity. But need it be the cessation of all the higher levels of activity in the bodily spiral? The human body is not just a biological machine. The biological cycles of activity are the expression of a relationship between a personal self and the world, and that same relationship gives rise to higher cycles of activity than the biological. It is not absurd to ask if the higher cycles of activity might not continue spiralling when the biological has come to an end and been left behind. To help the Corinthians envisage such a possibility, Paul points to the way a seed dies and makes a transition into the different body of the plant: ''But some one will ask, 'How are the dead raised? With what kind of body do they come?' You foolish man! What you sow does not come to life unless it dies. And what you sow is not the body which is to be, but a bare kernel, perhaps of wheat or of some other grain'' (I Cor 15:35-7). What is visible in death is the cessation of cycle after cycle of activity. What we anticipate in hope is the continuance and further development of the higher levels of the spiral of our bodily selves — bodily because still in relationship to the world and other persons.

An important practical consideration results from this conception of our bodily selves and their resurrection. At what level do we place our personal identity? Do we focus upon the cycle of eating and drinking? Or, if that is too crude for our taste, do we see life as a banquet and our aim to have our fill from its tables? What about the business of this world —. the making of money, the accumulation of property, the seeking of power? Is it at that level that we find the self we recognize as our own? The self is multi-levelled. If every level of activity we recognize and promote belongs to the perishable affairs of this world, which will cease at death, how do we expect to make sense of the resurrection? If we ignore and even block the higher cycles of activity, how can the resurrection be an object of our hope? Let us ask ourselves what there is in our present lives which is not essentially perishable or bound up with the passing scene of this world. If there is nothing now in our lives that is of imperishable value, there is no point in a resurrection. The resurrection is not a return to life as we now have it, which would be nonsensical. Do we want to eat and drink eternally? The resurrection is a spiralling upward of those higher cycles of activity, emergent already in this life, and due to find their full development hereafter. The Christian life may be seen as the forging of an identity that will survive death because it is rooted in cycles of activity that death does not destroy.

How one-sided, then, is the common view of aging! It sees aging as a process of gradual decay, and so it is from one standpoint. Cycles of activities cease or become weakened and less effective. But from another standpoint, aging is a process of growth, a gradual strengthening of those activities which are spiralling upwards into the new state of resurrection. It is sad to watch some people becoming sour and embittered as they age, seeing only the negative side of growing old, the loss of cycle after cycle of relationships and action, and not recognizing or fostering the other side, the growth into an imperishable relationship with God and into a communion with the dead as well as with the living. But it is indeed a wonderful experience to meet an old person who, with a joyful relationship with reality and with serenity and trust, is waiting in hope for the transition that death will bring. The sting of death is sin, namely the fixing of the centre of our lives upon what is perishable. But when the perishable puts on the imperishable, death will be swallowed up in victory (see I Cor 15:53–6). That victory begins as we age into the resurrection.

Tenderness versus Purity

What comes to mind when we think of purity? Cleanness, no doubt. Again, the state of being unmixed or all of a kind. But if we explore our thoughts for a while, we shall, I think, sooner or later come up with the idea of hardness. Purity is the hardness that resists adulteration or mixture or contamination. The hard clarity of a diamond, its flawless splendour, may serve as a symbol.

Purity implies division. It rests upon the separation of the clean from the unclean — from the foreign or strange, from any mixture, from what is different or other. Purity wields a sword, a sword as hard as a diamond and by its cleaving the pure is divided from the impure. What does not conform is put to the sword and destroyed, so that it may not pollute.

Much religion is a search for purity, for the security of clear and fixed boundaries. That is why it is often rightly associated with hardness, with an unyielding insistence upon the established norms.

The religious search for purity has taken various forms. In pre-scientific days a function of religion was to give a general account of the cosmos and in that way to provide a stable framework for the life of society. The manifold objects and events of experience were brought under a set of categories, so as to create a cosmic and social order. There is, however, never a perfect fit between our categories and reality. What escaped the classification and did not conform to the categories was dealt with as unclean, so that the ritual observance of a distinction between the clean and the unclean became a means of reinforcing the social and cosmic order. Today when religion is no longer expected to provide a cosmology, ritual laws of purity may still, as with the Jews, function to mark the boundaries and preserve the identity of a particular community or people.

In the sphere of beliefs, the religious search for purity becomes the insistence upon the singleness of true belief to the exclusion of any plurality or compromise. Orthodoxy is, in general, defined less by its positive content than by its opposition to the unorthodox. It is pure by its exclusiveness. For Christians the opposition is threefold: against the unbelief of the pagan or heathen, against the heresy of heterodox believers, and against refusal of Christ by the Jews. The heathen have been converted by the sword or slaughtered by it. The heretics have been burned with fire, another symbol of purity. The Jews have been kept apart, but subjected to periodic destruction as infected elements.

On their side, Muslims and Jews have proclaimed a fierce monotheism which excluded any plurality from God and prohibited images, regarding both the Christian Trinity and the prolific divine imagery of the Hindus as a defiling idolatry. Meanwhile, from the yoga of the Hindus came an ascetic search for purity. This was an attempt to purify oneself from the body and from bodily functions, with all bodily discharges regarded as unclean and sources of pollution. But Hindu yoga was not unique. In one form or other the ascetic search for purity has pervaded religious traditions throughout the world. Purity has been identified with the suppression or control or elimination of the body, with its bodily needs, its bodily desires and impulses, its bodily passions. Sexuality is renounced by virginity and celibacy, eating and drinking reduced to a minimum and controlled by fasting, bodily desires dampened by mortification, bodily passions suppressed in pursuit of the ideal of passionlessness or *apatheia*. As far as is possible, human life, it was thought, must be purged of the bodily or material, so as to release the spirit. What is spiritual is conceived as having an unchanging gem-like splendour. It is hard, not soft. Softness means a defiling sensuality, a lack of moral fibre, or a looseness of behaviour, an unsureness or unreliability of beliefs. The saints are the pure, the unwavering, the unyielding — the hard.

Now, I have no wish to condemn the search for purity. It represents the human need for order and for control — for the subordination of the lower to the higher in the multi-dimensional nature and life of human beings. All the same, it should be recognized that an unbalanced stress upon purity has had destructively inhuman consequences. In the fifteenth and sixteenth centuries Spain was ravaged by an obsession with racial and religious purity which led to the hounding of Jews and Muslims and of any with mixed blood and to a ruthless rooting out of heretics. Racial prejudice is still with us, and people have not ceased to reinforce it with religion. In a more hidden fashion, fear of the body in the name of religion has warped the lives of many. But my purpose, I repeat, is not to mount an attack upon the religious search for purity. Instead, I want to present another contrasting side of religion, one much more in accord with the original spirit of Christianity than a stress upon purity, namely the surrender to tenderness.

Tenderness may be described as the softness that remains open to the impact of the other. The phrase "the other" is important here. It distinguishes the softness of true tenderness from the softness of mere flabbiness or weakness. The flabby are not genuinely sensitive to the other, they do not register the distinctive impact of the other, because all is lost in the formless confusion of the uncaring. The tender do care. They are sufficiently self-aware to care for themselves, in the sense of being responsive to their own distinctive qualities and needs. But as tender, they care for others. They are responsive to others, and in being responsive to others, they are prepared to receive from others, to appreciate their qualities, and to feel their needs as demands. Tenderness is not the plasticity of the immature, but the differentiated sensitivity of the fully developed.

All the same, the stress is on process, not on achievement. True responsiveness to the actual conditions of human existence evokes compassion and calls for forgiveness. Human life is messy. It never fits a pattern perfectly. Tender caring copes with the stubborn messiness of life, not by constant purging, not by ever harsher discipline, but by fostering growth in its tiniest manifestations.

If purity implies division, tenderness implies communion. It is tender affection that unites parents and children, husband and wife. It is tender affection that gives rise to a compassionate social concern and to the acceptance of plurality in unity, that is of community. Purity fears, indeed abominates, the hybrid or what is mixed, because it does not conform to our categories and classes. The hybrid becomes the unclean, the corrupt, the inferior. Purity knows only the closed unity of the single, the unmixed.

Tenderness is open to change, and is able to integrate the contribution of the other. It is not afraid of the hybrid, the mixed, provided the contribution of each is respected, so that communion produces synthesis, not confusion. Tenderness refuses to make our tidy divisions absolute. It seeks a creative communion of opposites, not their separation.

The body has much to do with all this. Body means relationship. Bodiliness is the characteristic of our spirit when it is inserted into nature and into the unity of the human species. It relates us to all other living beings and to inanimate nature and it provides the framework of our lives. It relates us to all human beings, because human life, both physically and culturally, is essentially one, embracing past and future generations, as well as our own. To fear the body is to fear relationships. The failure to appreciate bodiliness, with the tender responsiveness it brings, has made modern life so harsh, and made human beings coldly destructive of their own species, of other living beings, and of inanimate nature itself.

We live in a hard world of disembodied rationality and of mechanical rhythms. People want to avoid getting hurt. They seek invulnerability by grasping after positions of power or by restricting their involvement. Both domination and withdrawal result in a rigid unresponsiveness. To be bodily persons is to be vulnerable. The cost of a tender sensitivity is suffering. But without it there is no joy.

It would be special pleading simply to say that Christianity was a religion of tenderness, not of purity. Christian history is full of ambiguities. There were times and places when a drive for purity caused a monstrous insensitivity to the other and a suppression of the variety of human thought and experience. Fear of the body has played no small part in those excesses. All the same, it is true to say that, taken as a whole, the Christian tradition puts a high evaluation on the tender responsiveness of love and a low evaluation on the search for purity.

Admittedly, the God of Christians is still the Warrior-God of Israel, destroying enemies and punishing his own people for their unfaithfulness. Nevertheless, in the Old Testament there are also passages of great tenderness, such as these from Hosea and Isaiah, which compare God's love to that of a mother for her child:

Yet it was I who taught Ephraim to walk
I took them up in my arms;
but they did not know that I healed them.
I led them with cords of compassion,
with the hands of love,
and I became to them as one
who eases the yoke on their jaws,
and I bent down to them and fed them. (Hos 11:3–4)

Can a woman forget her sucking child,
that she should have compassion on the sons of her womb?
Even these may forget, yet I will not forget you. (Is 49:15)

That note of tenderness is picked up by the Book of Revelation, in many respects the supreme expression in the New Testament of the concept of God as a God of wrath. In it we read:

Behold, the dwelling of God is with men. He will dwell with them, and they shall be his people, and God himself will be with them; he will wipe away every tear from their eyes, and death shall be no more, neither shall there be mourning nor crying nor pain any more, for the former things have passed away. (Rev 21:3–4)

But far more decisive than any of these descriptions for the Christian exaltation of tenderness as a divine attribute is the fact of Jesus Christ. Because Jesus is the Son of God, the Second Person of the Trinity, made man for us, the sufferings of Jesus were the sufferings of God. It was God in Christ who suffered with us and for us. He came down to share our vulnerability. To do so corresponded to the very nature of the Godhead. Christians worship a responsive, suffering God, not an impassible Absolute.

Christianity, the religion of the God-man, does not fear the hybrid or the plural. It has modified the pure monotheism that proclaims the singleness of the Godhead against any plurality or relationships within. For Christian believers in the Trinity, plurality and relationships are not just signs of finitude; they belong to Ultimate Reality. And the plurality within the Godhead manifests itself in a divine self-giving to human beings. The divine Thought within the Godhead becomes the Word made flesh, that is, the divine Thought is given body within human history. The divine Love or Holy Spirit becomes the Gift sent by the risen Jesus, that is, the divine Love is made present in the Christian community as an unending source of self-giving love. To believe in the Trinity is to conceive the inner life of the Godhead, with its plurality and unity, as the counterpart and model of the way of life constitutive of the Christian community — a life of relationships and of self-giving love.

That way of life we find exemplified in the earthly life of Jesus. He refused to make the pursuit of purity a paramount concern. He was prepared to leave aside the ceremonial laws of purity and the law of the sabbath when compassion or the fostering of human relationships demanded it. He mixed with tax-collectors, prostitutes, and other sinners. He went so far as to eat with them, ignoring social distinctions and the socially engendered fear of contamination. Positively, he made himself vulnerable by continuing with his teaching and his way of acting, despite the opposition it aroused. He was put to death because his attitude was subversive of the established order, and he could conform only by closing his heart to the call and needs of others. He preferred a flexible responsiveness to keeping intact the categories and norms of the social and religious order.

A fear of tenderness pervades present society, stunting personal and social development.Only the suppression of tenderness can explain the frozen insensititivy and absence of human responsiveness so frequently manifested by those with decision-making power in our society. That blighting fear of tenderness can be reinforced by religion. Its expression is to be found in religious dogmatism and moral absolutism. Religion can become a one-sided striving after purity, which cannot abide the intractable messiness of life and its teeming, unclassifiable variety. But true purity is not achieved by restriction. ''To the pure all things are pure'' (Tt 1:15), and inner purity has its source in love.

The Individual and Community

When Paul is dealing with the Church as the body of Christ, he puts before us two complementary truths. For example, take the fourth chapter of the Letter to the Ephesians. He tells us that "grace was given to each of us according to the measure of Christ's gift" (v.7). Each one of us, then, has his or her individual gift. Yet all these gifts are "for the building up the body of Christ" (v.12), and "there is one body and one Spirit" (v.4). The first truth, therefore, is that each of us is addressed by God as an individual with a unique vocation and a unique set of gifts. The second truth is that the individual vocation and the individual set of gifts are for the building up of the one community of salvation. Individual and community: two essential poles of Christian, indeed of human life. It all sounds banal. We have heard it so often before. But that does not make it less important. Let us try to deepen our understanding of what is involved.

Let us begin with individuality as the opposite pole to community. What it means to be an individual may be grasped in a negative fashion. To be an individual is to experience an essential loneliness. That this is so may be shown by considering how death is inevitably an individual, lonely event. No one can die for us or with us. We die alone, even if we are surrounded in our dying by loving relatives and friends. But death is an individual event because of a wider truth. No one can take over the heart of my consciousness and produce for me or on my behalf my basic response to reality. For that reason, the salvation of each of us is unique and individual. No one can elicit for me my act of faith and love. Each of us has individually to walk through the gate that gives access to eternal life. We may be encouraged by others, strengthened by their prayers, but then we have to go forward alone. My individuality is not limited to my death, in which I stand alone before the judgement-seat of God, but applies also to my basic response to God in this life.

Yet, that is not the whole truth even about my individuality. Individuality at the human level is not brute fact, but a process and a gift. We become individuals as we enter into our freedom as persons, and we become free by God's gift of salvation. We are not first individuals and then in a second instance called by God. Spiritually what makes us individuals is the call of God. God calls out each of us by name — Mary, Martha, Philip, James, and so on. By his call, we are unique persons, each with a distinct destiny. We stand each of us alone before God, answerable to him in a way that no one else can answer for us. We have our own faith and our own love, given to each of us as unique persons by the gift of God.

Each life, therefore, has a unique trajectory. There is no class, no category that can encompass our individuality. To give way to jealousy or envy is to be deluded by an abstraction. It is to suppose that we could be someone other than we are. The very same gifts that another has would not mean the same or have the same effect in the different concrete constellation of our own individuality. That individuality is a gift from God, our creator and redeemer. To recognize our essential uniqueness under the call of God is to reach an identity and freedom as a human person that cannot be taken away by any power on earth.

If now we turn to the other pole, community, we meet a paradox: the becoming of individuals is the very creation of community. It is not enough to say that community is necessary for the formation and education of individuals. True as that is, it does not go deep enough. To do so one has to say that the very achievement of the freedom and unique individuality of each person is identical with the achievement of community. Why is that so?

At a first level the answer is that the same call of God which confers spiritual individuality upon each of us is a call to enter into community — the new community of salvation. We are called to enter into the kingdom of God or to become members of the body of Christ. In the new community, ''there is neither Jew nor Greek, there is neither slave nor free, there is neither male nor female; for you are all one in Christ Jesus'' (Gal 3:28). The same call that makes each of us individuals with a unique destiny abolishes all distinctions in a union with Christ. God's call places us in a tension between the two poles of individuality and community, and both must be sustained.

At a second level we may ask why God calls us in that fashion. The reason is that becoming an individual in the distinctively human or spiritual mode demands self-transcendence. In other words, to become an individual with personal freedom, one must break out of the circle of self-centredness and find one's centre in the mysterious reality beyond the self.

Let me first put it in a somewhat abstract but comprehensible way. Human life is a quest for truth, goodness, and beauty. What is true, however, is not to be measured by what is of advantage to the self; we must go beyond selfish interest to find the truth. What is good is not assessed by the satisfaction of the self; we must go beyond selfish desires to find the good. What is beautiful is not limited to what pleases the taste of the self; we must go beyond selfish pleasure to find beauty. To refuse to go beyond the self is to enclose oneself in an illusory self-sufficiency and to relate to others merely in a relationship of manipulative domination because we are unable to acknowledge their distinctive reality. We lose our freedom and our individuality because we are self-enclosed. To become our true selves, we have to be fearlessly open to the whole of reality — to God, to others, to every manifestation of truth, goodness, and beauty in the world.

In brief, we have to go beyond the self to find the self. The process of self-realization is a quest for truth, goodness, and beauty which transcend the self. Self-realization is self-transcendence. But in that self-transcendence, the self joins other selves. All selves are united in finding their centre outside themselves in a common tension towards truth, goodness, and beauty. The very movement of self-transcendence that gives us our freedom and individuality unites us to other selves in community or common sharing.

Let me put it in another way. The human self is esentially inter-subjective. I mean that, prior to the organization of community and the establishment of common institutions, the self is united in a vital union with other selves. The vital oneness of the self with other selves, prior to any particular social organization, means that to actualize the self is to actualize community. The two processes of realization coincide. The becoming of the individual is the very creation of community.

Genuine human community arises from free subjects. Individualism is usually taken to mean that there is no law higher than the individual, so that the individual is the sole source and bearer of meaning and value. But there is another understanding. According to that, the basis of individuality is the response to the call of God, and human community has the same transcendent origin and basis. God in calling out individuals calls them into community. That community of free individuals is the kingdom of God, only found imperfectly in partial manifestations in this life. It cannot be identified completely with any institution or social organization, secular or ecclesiastical. But that does not mean it is not a reality with a powerful presence within this world and history. It is present as a community-forming force, leading men and women again and again to take up the work of creating human communities.

To make this rather high-flown reflection more concrete, I want to distinguish between a politics of power and a politics of communication. At the basis of the distinction is the contrast between two different kinds of action, two different ways in which we relate to other persons.

The first kind of action is a unilateral action by which a person manipulates the world and other people in order to shape reality and society to serve his or her individual self-interest. Its aim is control. It is an exercise of power. Other people are used simply as means in pursuit of one's own interests. All this leads to a form of politics in which society is seen as an aggregate of individuals, each pursuing selfish interests, and the order that arises out of the resulting conflict is simply a balance of power, with the stronger groups achieving domination of the weaker and an uneasy equilibrium of tension amongst themselves.

The second kind of action in which human beings relate to one another may be called communicative action. This does not aim at success in manipulating the reality of other people to one's own purposes. The aim instead is mutual understanding and agreement. When people relate together in that way, seeking reciprocal understanding and not domination, an order emerges out of the network of communication, an order in which everyone participates. It is not the success of a single party or view, but the creation of something new — a genuinely new order. Communicative action, which renounces domination and fearlessly opens oneself to the thoughts and aspirations of others, gives rise to a different kind of politics or search for social order — a search for genuine community.

Now, communicative action when analysed implies a demand for self-transcendence on the part of human beings as moral agents and that self-transendence remains a utopian dream unless our pursuit of truth and the good, our human reason, is a participation in a transcendent order. Human history is indeed largely the story of the politics of power, but with a constant manifestation of the human longing for a social order based upon communication among free persons. Why does such longing remain frustrated? Because, while some measure of communicative action is inseparable from our humanity, to become radically free as individuals and open to others in community, we have to step out of the enclosed circle of our self-interest and relate to God as the transcendent centre of our being and our lives. But that means we are dealing with the mystery of God's grace and human sinfulness. Community and individuality in their fullness are the effect of God's grace, but on account of human sinfulness they are realized only imperfectly in history.

If there is one witness that is needed from Christians today, it is the witness of genuine community, which includes genuine individuality and freedom. The world is seeking a way out of its politics of power, which are leading to annihilation. Unfortunately, the churches seem more concerned to preserve the tattered remnants of a past social order than to show how to create a new one. They should be preaching the kingdom of God, which in literal terms means community, individuality, and freedom, based upon the love of a transcendent God.

Water into Wine

The Gospel of John exhibits the reality of salvation differently from the other gospels. They see it as a future reality. The kingdom is indeed at hand, but yet it is still to come. For John it is a reality already present. There is no final contradiction, because neither account of salvation is intended as exclusive; it is a matter of emphasis. Nevertheless, it is worth reflecting upon John's presentation of the judgement of the world as already taking place, of the glorification of Jesus as already being done, of eternal life as already given. "Now is the judgement of this world, now shall the ruler of this world be cast out" (Jn 12:31). "The hour has come for the Son of man to be glorified" (Jn 12:23). "Truly, truly, I say to you he who hears my word and believes him who sent me, has eternal life; he does not come into judgement, but has passed from death to life" (Jn 5:24).

With a play on words, John presents the very death of Christ, his lifting up on the cross in the crucifixion, as the exaltation of Christ, his lifting up in glory. " 'And I, when I am lifted up from the earth, will draw all men to myself.' He said this to show by what death he was to die" (Jn 12:31-2). The hour of his death was the very hour of his glorification. The death and resurrection of Christ are seen, not as separate events, but as the same. "Father, the hour has come; glorify thy Son that thy Son may glorify thee" (Jn 17:1). "And now, Father, glorify thou me in thy own presence with the glory which I had with thee before the world was made" (Jn 17:5). For John, Jesus from the begining of his earthly existence had the glory that belonged to him as the Son of the Father. That glory was hidden, but made manifest in various ways. Miracles were one of the manifestations. They were signs, showing forth his glory. Of the first of the miracles, the changing of water into wine at the marriage feast of Cana, it is said: "This, the first of his signs, Jesus did at Cana in Galilee, and manifested his glory; and his disciples believed in him" (Jn 2:11). The meaning of that miracle is the teaching I have been drawing from John's Gospel as a whole, namely that salvation is a present reality. The vast quantity of water turned into wine, no less than one hundred and twenty gallons, is intended to teach that the abundance promised for the messianic age is already here.

What, then, in simple words, is the point I am trying to make from John's Gospel? It is that our true life is not something to come in the future, but something we have here and now. We already enjoy eternal life. If that does not seem to be so, it is because we have the wrong attitude and are misconceiving our own present existence. How, then, does John's teaching work out in practice?

"Fill the jars with water." Our ordinary lives are like the water with which Jesus began at the marriage feast of Cana. At times we ask ourselves, "Is this all there is?" Let us go over in our minds the ordinary routine of life. Some few of us have interesting jobs, but even then there are long stretches of tedium and boredom. Others are locked for years in jobs that have little or no meaning or interest. And those are the lucky ones. There are those without a job, the unemployed, who are refused even the minimum function in the work of society. For everyone there is a multitude of trivial tasks to be got through every day. Personal relationships do give richness and meaning to our lives, but they are subject to many ups and downs, and their failure is frequently experienced. In our society where people are constantly moving around, many find themselves eventually isolated, without friends or relatives nearby. Once youth is past, life soon gives the impressions of not getting anywhere. "O God, is there nothing more than this?" we say to ourselves. Everyone is indeed busy, but at points where life is truly meaningful, we do not say that we're busy. Do we ever say, "I'm busy listening to this symphony," or, "I'm busy making love"? We are busy when what we are doing has no particular meaning. Our lives are water. Will they be turned into wine?

What are some of the ways in which people try to give some meaning to their lives?

The first, and perhaps the most common, is to retreat into a dream of fulfilment. Harlequin romances sell by the million. The longing they express is real, but the fulfilment is unreal. Hence they cannot in the end give real satisfaction. Their religious equivalent, equally unreal, is a hope for a future heaven when that hope has no basis in this life and that heaven is not a completion of this life, but simply succeeds and replaces it.

Another way we try to give meaning to our lives is to look for rescue from above. This is the apocalyptic expectation which constantly recurs in history. The Book of Revelation in the New Testament is one example of it. This world will be destroyed, and there will be a new heaven and a new earth. God "will wipe away every tear from their eyes, and death shall be no more, neither shall there be mourning nor crying nor pain any more, for the former things have passed away" (Rev 21:4).

The modern version of the apocalyptic expectation is found in science fiction, with its theme of rescue from outer space. There are two types of science fiction. In the first, the future arises out of the present without any essential change. There are the same wars, the same problems and conflicts, the same good and evil people, but now with new gadgets and weapons. That type of science fiction is exemplified by *Star Wars*. In the other type, a new reality, found in outer space, will come as a gift to the human race, lifting it on to a new plane. Here, indeed, we do not have simply an extension into outer space of our present unsatisfactory life on earth, but the incursion of something new which will rescue us from our present impasse. Examples of that kind of science fiction are *E.T., 2001*, and *Close Encounters of the Third Kind*.

There is some truth in the apocalyptic expectation. We do look for rescue from above. Salvation does come as a gift from beyond the human race and its resources. But apocalyptic imagery does not work with us as it did before. The reason is what may be called the "black apocalypse." The destruction of this present world is most likely to occur through a nuclear war, and the other side of nuclear destruction is not resurrection, but nothingness. When earlier generations thought in dramatic terms of the cessation of this world, they thought of transformation, of renewal, of a new order rising out of the old. For us, the final battle or Armageddon will bring annihilation, nothing, final death. We cannot think beyond the destruction because our feverish preparation for self-destruction has emptied the present of meaning, and hope can be built only upon a meaningful present.

"Now draw some out and take it to the steward of the feast." When we open ourselves to God in love at the command of Jesus, our ordinary lives are changed into wine. Without visible commotion or without any striking change in the circumstances and routines of our lives, they manifest the glory of God. They become the expression of the creative love, goodness, and glory at the heart of all reality and of human history. The difference lies at the level at which we grasp the reality of life.

How different life can look according to the depth of our vision! I shop regularly at a local supermarket which is near enough for me to use a shopping cart. As I stood outside one busy day, with a cart full of groceries, I suddenly saw the whole scene as something out of the *Arabian Nights*: the display of goods from every part of the world, the colourful clothes, the many cars as miracles of modern engineering, all the people, each person a marvel of memories, longings, capacity for love, destined to be companions for eternity in the life of God. Then, just as suddenly, the vision faded, and I saw myself as a tired and somewhat harassed man, dragging a heavy cart of groceries through dirty streets amid clouds of exhaust fumes, pushing my way through crowds of people, each one pursuing selfish interests and ignoring everyone else. Which perception is the true one? At one level both are true. The question is, Which is the final truth about human existence? Without faith, the perception that sees life as pointless and tawdry and selfish seems the only one in touch with reality and the perception of life as wonderful and rich and fulfilling as an unreal vision. With faith, it is like being asked simply to wipe the mud off a precious stone to uncover the glowing beauty beneath. The so-called realists are just unperceptive children who preferred to mess about in the mud.

Am I saying that whether our lives are water or wine is simply a matter of the way we look at life? Our lives remain substantially the same, but our attitude to them changes? Yes and no. It is a question of our attitude, but our attitude does substantially change our lives. The nearest analogy is that of falling in love. When we are deeply in love, it transforms our whole existence. Every element in our life takes on a new meaning. To be in love leads us to make changes in what we do, in the substantial content of our life, but the fundamental change is within, in our attitude, in our heart. Likewise with faith, which is an opening of ourselves in love to God. The felt presence of the reality of God as love transforms our whole existence, turns the water of our life into wine. We do indeed make changes in what we do, in what we think, in the circumstances and routines by which we live, but the fundamental change is our inner openness to the Spirit of Love. This gives us a joy that nothing can take from us, the beginning here and now of eternal life, the resurrection that is present in death itself.

Let me come back to the insight found in John's Gospel that salvation is a present reality. In stressing the here-and-now presence of eternal life, John does not deny a future fulfilment. The point at issue is whether we see the future as built upon the present or the present as built upon the future. The second alternative plunges us into unreality — into a rejection of this life, into feverish efforts to escape it, into a perception of this existence as worthless mud. The first alternative recognizes the deep and wonderful reality beneath the mud of this life — the love, the joy, the glory found in humankind. Truly we are looking for the full release of that glory, but already from Christ, ''from his fullness have we all received, grace upon grace'' (Jn 1:16).

God Is the Other

In the Gospel of Luke, immediately after the return to Galilee from the fasting and temptation in the desert, comes the story of the rejection of Jesus by the people of his own town, Nazareth (Lk 4:14–28). In response to their unbelief, Jesus reinforces his message by two further points, and what he says makes his hearers so angry that they try to kill him by throwing him over the nearby cliff. The two points made by Jesus, which were so unpalatable to his audience, were, first, that no prophet is acceptable in his own country, and, second, that strangers are closer to God than members of the chosen people. Let us dwell on each point in turn.

No prophet is acceptable in his own country. Metaphorically, the people of Jesus' own country are religious people — those who are conventionally religious. People who are privileged religiously often become deaf to the Word of God. Religion can be used as the most effective way of avoiding God. It can serve as a kind of inoculation against the threat or challenge of God's demanding call. By going to church on Sundays, saying a few prayers, and keeping the more obvious commandments or at least acknowledging one's guilt and asking for pardon afterwards, one can continue to live one's ordinary life in the world without further upset from religion.

But God's Word will not be domesticated in that way. When it comes upon us with its prophetic force, it is upsetting and subversive. It does not fit into the quiet, domestic order we have made our own country. If listened to, God's Word prevents our settling down in a comfortable state of satisfaction with ourselves and our lives. Note these texts:

> For the word of God is living and active, sharper than any two-edged sword, piercing to the division of soul and spirit, of joints and marrow, and discerning the thoughts and intentions of the heart. And before him no creature is hidden, but all are open and laid bare to the eyes of him with whom we have to do. (Heb 4:12–13)

I know your works; you have the name of being alive, and you are dead. Awake, and strengthen what remains and is on the point of death, for I have not found your works perfect in the sight of my God. Remember then what you received and heard; keep that, and repent. If you will not awake, I will come like a thief, and you will not know at what hour I will come upon you. (Rev 3:1-3)

I know your works: you are neither cold nor hot, would that you were cold or hot! So, because you are lukewarm, and neither cold nor hot, I will spew you out of my mouth. (Rev 3:15)

These texts do not support the assumption that the Word of God can be tamed into a tranquil respectability. We can add the parable of the wedding feast (Mt 22:1-10: Lk 14:16-24). Those invited did not answer the invitation, but made excuses. In the end none of those invited shared in the feast, but people were gathered from the highways and byways. Even more shocking, though familiarity has blunted its impact, is the saying that prostitutes and tax-collectors will go into the kingdom before those esteemed good (Mt 21:32).

In brief, cannot we sum up the first point by saying that if we are comfortable with the Word of God, we are not in fact listening to it?

One might indeed protest, "Surely, the Word of God does give comfort." Yes; but there is a paradox here. If we risk everything and emerge from the shell of human security we have formed for ourselves, we will find genuine comfort and contentment. "He who finds his life will lose it, and he who loses his life for my sake will find it"(Mt 10:39). If we look back upon our own lives, we shall see, I am sure, many opportunities missed and true contentment threatened or postponed because we were pusillanimous, afraid to take a risk, not in fact open to the challenge of the Word of God.

The second point, that strangers are closer to God than members of the chosen people, is more difficult to make one's own. Put in a universal form, it means that to find God we must find him in the other, in the stranger. Racial prejudice, nationalist prejudice, religious prejudice — these are denials of God. But the point here is not a moral one. It is not that we have a moral obligation to love our neighbour, to be benevolent and do good to all human persons. It goes deeper than that. God is the other, the stranger, because of his transcendence. Transcendence is by very definition otherness. We cannot meet God unless we open ourselves to his otherness.

It is much easier to accept the otherness of human strangers than it is to accept the divine otherness. If one cannot achieve the lesser self-opening, how will one achieve the greater? The First Letter of John makes the same point in more familiar language: ''If any one says, 'I love God,' and hates his brother, he is a liar; for he who does not love his brother whom he has seen, cannot love God whom he has not seen'' (1 Jn 4:20). A person who is eaten up with racial prejudice or who regards all foreigners as inferior or who despises people of another class reveals an absence of the spiritual capacity to meet God, the Supreme Other. The extent to which we accept the created otherness of human persons is the extent to which we are open to the uncreated otherness of God. The extent to which we close ourselves to the stranger is the extent to which we are refusing God.

There is indeed a problem of the other, namely a problem of the relationship between the self and the other. How can we relate to the other as other, without, in relating the other to the self, reducing the other to the self, drawing the other into the circle of our selfhood? On the other hand, if we relate to the other as irreducibly other, how can we do so without plunging into a self-alienation which estranges ourselves from ourselves? Philosophers discuss the problem of the other, but let me put it here in simpler language. How can we learn from another culture without bending and twisting that culture so that it fits in with our own? Or, how can we enter into another culture without diluting our own or losing our own distinctive identity? Can we become bicultural or bilingual without dividing the self?

The answer to the problem lies in the very nature of the self as a capacity for relationships. The objection conceives the self as a closed entity, threatened in its identity by any intrusion from outside. But such a self is a secondary construction which has to be dismantled to find the true self. The true self is openness, relatedness, a capacity to become all things, a desire for the other, essentially for the Supreme Other, God.

Hence it is understandable that Christ came as the stranger. The text, "And the Word became flesh and dwelt among us" is translated more literally as, "And the Word became flesh and pitched his tent among us" (Jn 1:14). He lived among his own people as one who had no home: "Foxes have holes and birds of the air have nests; but the Son of man has nowhere to lay his head" (Mt 8:20). Jesus thus acted out the message he brought, which was, as he told the people of his own town of Nazareth, if you cannot see God in the stranger, you will not find him in your synagogues — let us say, in our churches.

It is well to remind ourselves of that message in these days when there are many strangers in our midst and when these strangers are so often perceived as a threat to the rickety, insecure selves we have erected to enclose our true selves. Our true self is a capacity for the other — immediately for the created other or human stranger, mediately through the human stranger to the uncreated other, God.

Living as Pilgrims

We should live, not as victims nor as fanatics, but as pilgrims. What does that mean?

In the Epistle to the Hebrews we read: "By faith we understand that the world was created by the word of God, so that what is seen was made out of things which do not appear" (Hb 11:3). The text contrasts visible reality, "what is seen" and invisible reality, "things which do not appear." Invisible reality is the source of the visible reality, and visible reality is the result or effect of the invisible. Faith is the bridge between the two. As we read in the same chapter of Hebrews, "Now faith is the assurance of things hoped for, the conviction of things not seen" (Hb 11:1).

By faith we live in the in-between; in other words, in the tension between visible and invisible realities, belonging to both, acknowledging both, but drawn towards the invisible.

Victims are those who live immersed in the visible, so that they are without the invisible. Fanatics are those who try to live in the invisible alone, denying, rejecting, ignoring the visible. Pilgrims are those who move to the invisible, but who find it in, through, and under the visible.

Victims, people who try to live without the invisible, become victims in different ways. They may be victims of history, victims of society, victims of other people, or victims of themselves.

To live without the invisible is to live without the assurance of things hoped for, that is, without any sense of a providential guidance watching over the human race. History is just one thing after another in a meaningless succession. In Shakespeare's words, "it is a tale told by an idiot; signifying nothing." Those without faith or hope are lost in a flux of events without direction or purpose. They are victims of unintelligible forces in the visible order, and they exclude any invisible source of meaning.

In that situation many look to society or the state as the only reality transcending the individual. They become victims of society, locked in the various nationalisms and particularisms for which individuals of our time have been slaughtered by the million. The crisis of modernity does not lie in the vision of humanity it claims as its own, but the lack of correspondence between that vision and the experienced reality of twentieth-century life. The vision modernity claims is that of the autonomous self and free individual. The reality is that of the unparalleled slaughter of millions in the name of different collectivities and collective ideologies.

The only protection against the absorption of the self into a collectivity is the relation of that self to the transcendent God. It is that relationship that establishes for each person an autonomous space where the intimate being of the self opens out on to a reality that transcends the temporal order and society. If the human subject has no such transcendent relationship at the core, it is difficult to see why the individual should not be abolished as a now obsolete form of human existence and replaced by a more efficient scientific control of social behaviour. We should all then as individuals be victims sacrificed on the altar of Leviathan — the brave new world of the scientifically administered society.

The beginning of both the Jewish and the Christian traditions is identified with Abraham's going out of Ur of the Chaldees and making himself an exile, a pilgrim. As we read in Genesis: "Now the Lord said to Abram, 'Go from your country and your kindred and your father's house to the land that I will show you' " (Gen 12:1). The Epistle to the Hebrews gives us a comment upon Abraham's action: "By faith Abraham obeyed when he was called to go out to a place which he was to receive as an inheritance; and he went out, not knowing where he was to go. By faith he sojourned in the land of promise, as in a foreign land, living in tents with Isaac and Jacob, heirs with him of the same promise. For he looked forward to the city which has foundations, whose builder and maker is God" (Hb 11:9-10). Abraham was able to free himself from the embrace of the society in which he had been born and bred because he was called out by the invisible God. He is for us a symbol that our only release from the smothering hug of collectivities based on instinct into personal autonomy and a society based on freedom is the relationship with a transcendent God who calls us out by his promise.

Abraham was not a victim because he lived by the invisible reality of God and the invisible reality of a city of promise which did not yet exist. I have said that victims are those who lived immersed in the visible. As well as being victims of history and of society, they become victims of other people.

Without the tension of living in the in-between, drawn towards the invisible, personal relations of any depth are impossible. If there is no reality other than the tangible, what motivation is there other than self-interest? Hence people simply exploit one another for their own purposes. We all prey on one another, become victims of one another, in what is not so much a society but a rat race, controlled by those able to dominate by force.

If we become victims, exploited by one another, we are also victims of ourselves, of our own impulses. Unless we allow ourselves to be drawn towards the invisible and thus establish an orientation or direction in our lives, what is there to create an order among the desires, drives, interests, and needs that pull us in every direction? We become passive victims of our own complex nature. It is faith in invisible reality that enables us to move forward to our destiny.

If victims are those who live imprisoned in the visible because they have no faith in the invisible, fanatics represent the other extreme, namely, those who want the invisible by itself, without the visible. Fanatics try to purify themselves from any involvement with the visible, the tangible. They hate the body. Consequently, they seek to deny history and society. In doing so, they deny other people and deny themselves.

Fanatics deny history because they will not accept change. They are threatened by growth or development. They want a static world in which nothing changes. Why are religious fundamentalists so vehement in their rejection of evolution? It is because of their resistance, unconscious as well as conscious, to the idea and fact of change. They identify salvation with security, invisible reality with the exclusion of change, and they have not grasped the meaning of the Incarnation as the mediation of the invisible by the visible.

Fanaticism can also mean the denial of society. The empty cosmopolitanism so widespread today is a secularized version of religious fanaticism. Religion, whether in a traditional or in a secularized form, can take on a pseudo-universality, with a denial of its roots in a particular time and place and culture. The uprootedness of people in modern Western society, the homogenization of culture, the unlimited mobility, the lack of ties to a particular community, the loss of a sense of place — all this is a mutated offspring of fanatical religion. We have all become nomads, but unlike Abraham we are nomads without a Promised Land. We have taken the absolute character of religion and wrongly made it a reason for denying the particularity of any genuinely human life.

Fanatics, both religious and secular, deny other people. Religious fanatics burn heretics. They do so because in the name of a religious cause they have suppressed the response of their own humanity to the humanity of the other person. They have understood the religious affirmation of the invisible as allowing the denial of our human feelings. They have justified their humanity by supposing that the bodiliness of our feelings allows us to trample them down.

Those who once burned heretics in the name of God now bomb villages in the name of democracy and freedom. The world is ruled today by people who are living out a secular version of the denial of the visible. Their attitude was summed up well by the remark of the American general in Vietnam who said that they had to destroy a Vietnamese village in order to save it. The concrete, particular reality of the visible world and the actual bodily reality of other persons are denied in the name of some absolute — abstract and invisible.

People who cannot come to terms with the visible world, with its limits and its changeability, and who suppress the response of their humanity to other human beings are in fact filled with self-hatred. They are unable to accept themselves, especially their bodily selves. Their denial of history, society, and other people is a manifestation of a failure to acknowledge the limited, bodily, changing, messy reality of their own human self. They identify themselves instead with a spiritual, crystalline, unchanging self — which in reality is an imaginary construct.

To deny the invisible is to live as a victim of the visible: to deny the visible is to falsify the invisible, conceiving it as a destructive tyranny rather than as a creative source. How does each of these extremes, first, confront the fact of death and, second, develop bodily personal relationships?

Some people die as victims. They struggle bitterly against a meaningless end. With no hope in the invisible, they can do nothing in the face of death as a destructive force. Others die as fanatics, denying the reality of death, pretending that death is not the end of human, personal existence as we know it. Religion can become a pretence, an attempt on our part to forget that to hope is to question with trust, not to be in possession of the answers. Religion does not remove the negative fact of death, nor does it give us knowledge of what lies beyond. The descriptions of the future life are expressions of our hope, not statements of our knowledge. What is it do die, not as a victim nor as a fanatic, but as a pilgrim? I read somewhere — I forget where — that we should die as seafarers, who greet with an equal eye the deep they are entering and the shore they are leaving. As pilgrims we live in the tension between the visible and invisible. So, in dying, we cast a lingering gaze upon the visible from which we are journeying, but then turn from it to the unknown towards which we are striving.

Part of the negative reality of death is the disruption it brings to the personal relationships that make up our lives as human beings. Those who live immersed in the visible are unable to develop deep relationships with others, because they are victims of their immediate impulses and desires. Sexual relationships are for them little more than animal copulation. There is nothing in their relationships that can meaningfully be thought of as surviving death. At the other extreme, fanatics who deny the visible in the name of the invisible are unable to develop and sustain truly human relationships because they find all bodily expression, particularly sexual, crude and distasteful. There is something inhuman in the way such people often claim to have a spiritual love of others, while devoid of any empathetic response to another's feelings, interests, or needs. The suppression of bodiliness leads to a closure against the reality of others. As human beings, we meet one another bodily or we do not meet at all. When we are intertwined with the reality of another person, death is a most painful sundering, even though we retain the assurance of hope and the conviction that we remain united through our communion together in the invisible reality of God.

As Christians we are called upon to live by faith and hope. Since faith is not vision and hope is not knowledge, we are called upon to live as pilgrims in the in-between. We live journeying towards the invisible reality, but in and through the visible reality that constitutes our path to the invisible. We are neither angels nor beasts, but bodily spirits, on pilgrimage towards a spiritual destiny that will bring bodily fulfilment.

"Whatever Became of Sin?"

Whatever Became of Sin? is the title of a book by the well-known psychiatrist, Dr. Karl Menninger, of the Menninger Foundation (Bantam, 1978). In it he pleads for a revival of a sense of sin, namely, a return to an acknowledgement of error, transgression, offense, and responsibility. He calls for a conscious sense of guilt and implicit and explicit repentance, and he regards such a return to sin as a reason for hope. A sense of sin would bring hope, because it implies both a possibility and an obligation for intervention. We are not left in a miasma of evil, victims of our situation, without the ability to do anything about it.

Certainly, one can make no sense of the Christian religion without giving a large place to sin. Immediately before the coming of Christ, the line of prophets which prepared the way for Christ was brought to its completion in the figure of John the Baptist. His message was a call to repentance. Jesus took up the same message: "The time is fulfilled, and the kingdom of God is at hand; repent, and believe in the gospel" (Mk 1:15). The gospel or good news is the forgiveness of sins for those who repent.

One can say without exaggeration that we are confronted today with two different and opposing visions of human life and freedom: the Christian and the modern. According to the Christian scheme of things, human beings are all sinners, entrapped under the power of sin and needing the grace of God's forgiveness if they are to overcome evil. For the typically modern person, human beings are fundamentally innocent, their faults and errors and the evil they bring about can be remedied by reform. No radical repentence or gift of forgiveness is required.

To sharpen the point, one can say that people today have no sense of sin, but are riddled with guilt. What is the difference between sin and guilt, in the sense I am using guilt here?

An awareness of sin implies the acknowledgement of a transcendent order, an order greater than the self, an order where the self is not the centre. Sin is a violation of a self-transcendent order. For that reason, paradoxically, the revelation of God in the coming of Christ was at the same time a revelation of our sinfulness. The greater our sense of God, the deeper our sense of sin. It is in the very process of God's forgiveness that we become aware of the evil of our sinfulness.

Because sin is the violation of a transcendent order, we cannot measure sin against our own responses. Sin is still sin even if we enjoy it; it is sin even if it brings a sense of self-fulfilment; it remains sin even if it seems to be good for us and for others. Conscience, by which we discern what is sinful, is a practical judgement made in the light of our knowledge of God's law and God's purposes. Like other types of practical judgement, conscience needs training and improves with use. Above all, it requires a fostering of our sense of God and of the Christian teachings and values through which that presence is mediated to us as Christians. Even if personal responsibility is diminished because of our ignorance or lack of Christian maturity, a sinful action remains sinful because its moral value is assessed against a transcendent order, not just against our personal self.

The difference between a sense of sin and a guilt-trip is that guilt is focused upon the self. People feel guilty because they are insecure. Lacking a firm identity, they shrink before any change, and they are uncomfortable about any deviation from the routine, the conventional, the usual. What originated as intelligible moral prescriptions have become irrational taboos. No longer related to a transcendent order, the taboos serve as a protection of a feeble, artificial identity and, in doing so, result in a rejection of the other, a fearful hatred of anything or anyone different.

Self-centred guilt has at different times ravaged human society. There was the pathological drive for purity in Spain from the fifteenth to the seventeenth century, leading to the expulsion of the Jews, the driving-out of the Moors, and the persecution of dissidents by the Spanish Inquisition. Then there were the witch-hunts all over Europe. In our own day we have experienced the irrational concern of the Nazis with the purity of a mythical Aryan race, and their attempt to exterminate the Jews and to enslave what they considered inferior races. Racial prejudice is still widespread today, and waves of hostility are provoked by the fear of homosexuals or communists or of any who deviate in any way from existing norms. Prejudice is the warding-off of the other, because the other is perceived as a threat to one's insecure identity. Encounter with the other arouses a deep sense of guilt; it threatens to uncover the conflicts within the self, one's own lack of conviction, the deception by which one hides from the self the fact that things are not as one pretends them to be.

With the many pathological manifestations of guilt, no wonder psychotherapists are generally reluctant to encourage a sense of sin or a conviction of sinfulness. But, I repeat, a sense of sin is not the same as self-centred guilt. I am not saying that sin itself is a good thing; that would be a contradiction. But I am saying that it is both healthy and morally good to acknowledge our sinfulness and need for forgiveness.

What, then, is sin? It is helpful to distinguish basic sin from sinful actions. Basic sin is the underlying defect, the manifestation of which is the sinful action. Basic sin is a failure to respond; it is a deadness, a lack of sufficient love, so that we do not rise to the challenge of the situation. Our love is not strong enough to meet the demands made upon us, so that the action we produce is defective and does not measure up to what is required.

For example, a married man is attracted to someone not his wife. His marriage has become a boring routine, and he is tempted by the excitement and seeming rejuvenation of an affair. The question is what will be his basic response to the challenge. Can he call upon sufficient love of God and the commitment that implies to higher values, such as chastity, fidelity, justice, and so on, to resist the temptation? Or, is that love moribund, half-dead, so that the failure to respond with sufficient strength results in the sinful action of adultery?

However, basic sin is manifested in less obvious forms. The love of God demands that we love our neighbour. In how many ways do Christians fail to meet that demand? We are constantly confronted, directly or indirectly, with evidence of poverty, unemployment, injustice, and oppression. We quieten our consciences by contributing to various charities, but do nothing to overcome the greed, the avarice, the acquisitiveness, the clinging to possessions, all of which have their roots in a fundamental selfishness, a basic failure in our love of God, which is not strong enough to bear fruit in a genuine love of others. We do not perceive our own deadness. Hence we are shocked when Jesus bluntly tells us. "How hard it is for those who have riches to enter the kingdom of God! For it is easier for a camel to go through the eye of a needle than for a rich man to enter the kingdom of God!" (Lk 18:24–5). More perhaps than anything else, preoccupation with possessions deadens our basic love of God and prevents us from living with the freedom and openness of children of God.

Caught in a web of sinfulness, we need a liberator. We do not have the power to redeem ourselves. How can we produce life and love out of our dead hearts? Forgiveness must come to us as a gift. People are often told to rouse up their good will. But the first step is to acknowledge one's sinfulness. The recognition of sinfulness, with the turning away from sin by repentence, is the beginning of our liberation, the sign that Jesus has come to us to bring life by his message and his grace into our inner deadness. As Jesus said, "Those who are well have no need of a physician, but those who are sick; I have not come to call the righteous, but sinners to repentance" (Lk 5:31–2).

ɔ

On Being Human

What does it mean to be a human being? A variety of conceptions of the human have succeeded one another in the history of culture.

Take, for example, the image of Renaissance Man. Shakespeare expresses it well in these words of Hamlet:

> What a piece of work is a man! How noble in reason! How infinite in faculty! in form, in moving, how express and admirable! in action how like an angel! in apprehension how like a god! the beauty of the world! the paragon of animals! And yet to me, what is this quintessence of dust? man delights not me; no, nor woman neither, though, by your smiling, you seem to say so. (Act II,2)

There is a contradiction here. Human beings are seen as noble, infinite, like gods; and, yet, in the final encounter they are said to disgust because of death. But our ability to accept death is a sign of our self-acceptance as human beings.

If we move forward two centuries from the Renaissance to the Enlightenment, we come to a different image and conception — one that is very much still with us. It is an image drawn by an age dominated by possessiveness and individualism. It pictures the human being as an independent, individual self-owner. Each person owns himself or herself, and is able to dispose of the self and its abilities and skills in the open market.

One must distinguish here between propaganda and the reality. According to the propaganda, human beings as autonomous, individual self-owners have become free and equal. The reality is the helplessness of isolation and a submission forced by the need to survive.

Freedom is understood in the individualistic conception as freedom from any dependence upon others. That means there are no given relationships. The only relationships are those entered into voluntarily with a view to one's own self-interest. Society becomes a crowd of individuals, each pursuing his or her own purposes, the state holding the ring and seeing that the rules are kept. But the isolated individual is not truly free. Human beings only flourish in community. Without community they remain stunted in growth and, despite the claptrap about freedom, the many remain exploited victims of the few who have achieved dominance.

A similar delusion distorts the understanding of equality. Equality may mean the putting right of injustice as, for example, when equal pay is demanded for equal work. Likewise, everyone should be equal before the law. Again, to take the deepest conception of equality, every person as a person is of unconditional worth and must always be treated as an end and never only as a means. All that is acceptable and true. But we are asked in the name of equality to be reconciled to a society without community, a social arena in which atomic individuals pursue their own self-interests with a merely manipulative relationship with others. This is a market conception of society, and it is defended on the grounds that everyone in it has an equal opportunity. We can all become millionaires if we work hard and use the opportunities we are given. There is a general's baton in every knapsack. Every boy can be an Abraham Lincoln and become president.

That version of equality is a lie, used to cover over an inhuman order of work and of economic exploitation. We are not all equal — certainly not in present society, nor is equality in the individualistic sense an ideal. To live a truly human life, to avoid isolation and helplessness, we must recognize our need for relationships and the dependence upon others those relationships bring. Not all forms of dependence imply a dominance-submission relationship. True community brings reciprocity not an asymmetrical dominance.

"It is not good that the man should be alone" (Gen 2:18). That statement of the need of each of us for the other immediately precedes the Genesis account of God's creation of Eve. The man/woman relationship may be taken as a basic form of human community. Like human relationships in general, it has been distorted into a dominance/submission relationship, which has violated the essential dignity and equality of all human beings.

Feminists have some reason for regarding patriarchy as the fundamental domination or oppression. But the answer does not lie in the rejection of all relationships and an assertion of a self-sufficient autonomy in a lonely struggle for self-fulfilment. (Nor do feminists think that. They look for a spiritual bonding among women in sisterhood, but to discuss that is beyond my present scope.) But what concerns me is that, owing to patriarchy and also to some forms of resistance to patriarchy, the man/woman relationship in our society has become infected with its pervasive individualism and its false conception of equality and freedom. One out of two marriages in the United States ends in divorce, one out of three in Great Britain. There is a sickness in our society, a sickness marked by a breakdown of all organic, stable relationships. We are all becoming separate, lonely, helpless individuals. Is that a genuine freedom? Is that the equality we want?

Let me introduce here the virtue of fidelity. There has been a loss of the ideal of fidelity. Fidelity is a steadfast acceptance of given relationships or bonds in the midst of difficulty, disillusionment, disappointment. I am not here arguing for an insistence upon laws as absolute. For example, I am not saying that divorce is always wrong, always a breach of fidelity. The finiteness and imperfection of human make-up and existence have always to be allowed for by the creation of exceptions to any norm or rule. But I cannot help observing how frequently the marital relationship is broken off when a greater measure of the virtue of fidelity would have allowed the couple to work through their difficulties into a new depth of love, respect, and mutual sympathy. Personal relationships today — the marriage relationship included — remain so often superficial because they are relinquished before difficulties have had time to work themselves out.

Fidelity is the acceptance of the given, the willingness not to question, except in extremity, the framework created by the combination of our involuntary situation and our past, voluntary commitments. People have the idea they can always start afresh, that they can enter a new phase, free from all their past failures and commitments. That is not so. Human life, both individually and historically, is cumulative. Fidelity is the virtue that allows us to cope with our inheritance. We do not jettison the given, but transform it. We constantly begin again, but not from scratch, but through a patient, active, transforming faithfulness to what we are and what we have previously undertaken.

What does it mean to be human? One thing it certainly means is to die. Not only human beings, but all living things die. What makes death human is that others share our dying. There is indeed a sense in which no one can share our death. Death is a lonely journey which we have to make on our own. Even if we are surrounded by those we love and who love us, death remains a uniquely personal event. All the same, death takes on a human aspect when it becomes an event within a community.

Who will be with us when we die? Who will remember us after we are dead? Those questions may well serve as a criterion of the human quality of our present life. If we can answer confidently my wife or my husband, my children or grandchildren, my relatives and friends, then we are living in the human fashion of community. If there is no one who will come to our dying, if there is no one who will remember us after we are dead, then something has gone wrong with us or with the society in which we have lived. It may not be our fault that we are left as isolated individuals with no one to care for us, but it certainly shows a lack of the dimension of human community in the world in which we have lived. The criterion, notice, applies even to very old people, who have through longevity survived the death of their parents, children, or friends. They should still in their old age have been integrated into a human community. If they die on their own without a caring community, it is a sign of a breakdown in human living. Our society, unfortunately, is one where many, many people die in the absence of anyone to whom they belong and who cares for them as their own. We have paid dearly for the pursuit of a wrongly conceived freedom and equality. Dependence is not identical to unfreedom. Equality in a lonely autonomy is not a human ideal.

The Incarnation gives us a lesson in true humanity. Confronted with the fact of human sin, God could have destroyed the human species and established something entirely new. It is that approach to the human problem which is symbolized in the story of Noah and the Flood. But God adopted a different solution. He accepted the given situation and worked from within to transform it. The principle underlying the Incarnation is stated very simply in the Epistle to the Hebrews: ''For because he himself has suffered and been tempted, he is able to help those who are tempted'' (Heb 2:18). Jesus Christ endured the consequences of human sin in order to initiate a process of reversal whereby that endurance would bring about a transformation of the situation and of its relationships.

Thus, the Incarnation is an illustration of patient fidelity. We need to follow its pattern in our lives. Without fidelity or the transformative acceptance of the given, there is no community. Without fidelity, there is no tradition. Without fidelity, there are only lonely individuals, whirling like atoms in empty space. Human pride has led to a notion of freedom and equality as meaning, ''You're on your own.'' But we cannot be human on our own.

Two in One Flesh

Marriage differs from the other six sacraments in not consisting of a sacred ritual. It is marriage itself, namely, the secular, worldly, natural reality which has been raised to the dignity of a sacrament. For centuries, the Church's ritual — the blessing of the union and so forth — was optional. Even now, though made necessary for the validity of the marriage, it is an added legal requirement, not the sacrament. The sacrament is still the marriage itself. The marriage is made up of the mutual consent, the consummation in sexual intercourse, and the permanent marital union.

Strangely enough, the first stage of the biblical tradition was marked by an insistence that marriage was not sacred. This insistence was directed against the fertility religions of Canaan, with their identification of God with the forces of life. In opposition to those religions, the biblical writers affirm the transcendence of God and his distinction from nature and the stream of fertility. Marriage for them was established by God the Creator, the author of nature. That is the bearing of both the accounts of the Creation in Genesis. The first, which is the later account, reads: "So God created man in his own image, in the image of God he created them; male and female he created them" (Gen 1:27). The second account says: "Therefore a man leaves his father and his mother and cleaves to his wife, and they become one flesh. And the man and his wife were both naked and were not ashamed" (Gen 2:24-5).

What is marriage as a secular reality, coming from God as the author of nature? It is a particular kind of personal union, mediated by sexual relations, in which a man and a woman share one life. It is the sharing of one life that distinguishes marriage from other personal relationships, such as friendship. Friends may be very close, but their lives remain distinct. To be friends they do not need to merge their daily lives into one life. In marriage, sexual relations establish a bodily unity of life which should open out into a complete sharing of lives. The sexual or the erotic side of marriage is directed to the achievement of personal union.

In the Bible, the Song of Songs conveys a view of erotic love and sexuality as a purely human reality. The sexual love is spiritualized, but it remains profane. It is not sacralized. The Song of Songs is a collection of lyric poems of sexual love. It was received into the biblical canon before it was given an allegorical interpretation, making it an expression of God's love for his people, Israel, and of the love of the soul or bride for God as the bridegroom. The first, basic, and literal meaning of the collection of lyrics is that of the creaturely goodness and joy of the man-woman relationship. Here is one of the poems:

How graceful are your feet in sandals,
O queenly maiden;
Your rounded thighs are like jewels,
the work of a master hand.
Your navel is a rounded bowl
that never lacks mixed wine.
Your belly is a heap of wheat,
encircled with lilies.
Your two breasts are like two fawns,
twins of a gazelle.
Your neck is like an ivory tower.
Your eyes are pools in Hesbon,
by the gate of Bath-rabbim.
Your nose is like a tower of Lebanon,
overlooking Damascus.
Your head crowns you like Carmel,
and your flowing locks are like purple;
a king is held captive in the tresses.

How fair and pleasant you are,
O loved one, delectable maiden!
You are stately as a palm tree,
and your breasts are like its clusters.
I say I will climb the palm tree
and lay hold of its branches.
Oh, may your breasts be like clusters of the vine,
and the scent of your breath like apples,

and your kisses like the best wine
that goes down smoothly.
gliding over lips and teeth. (Song 7:1-9)

The Song, as it is easy to see, celebrates the joy and splendour of human love. It is not afraid to express its erotic playfulness. Nevertheless, there is an underlying seriousness. Prior virginity is stressed (Song 8:8-12) and also the permanence of love: '' love is as strong as death. . . . Many waters cannot quench love, neither can floods drown it. If a man offered for love all the wealth of his house, it would be utterly scorned'' (Song 8:6-7).

To reduce marriage to a means of having children is a distortion of the human reality of sexual love. Marriage as a personal union does establish the appropriate context for having and educating children, but the marriage union is a reality independent from procreation. Fertility is not required for a valid marriage, even though for the marriage to be fertile is a blessing and gift upon the union, enriching and strengthening it. Marriage, in what it essentially is, persists after the children have grown up and gone from parents, leaving them once more on their own. The essence of marriage as an all -embracing sharing of life, both bodily and spiritual, means that marriage is rooted in our biological existence. For that reason, procreation and marital union are linked. But they are not the same and they can exist separately: procreation without marital union and marital union without procreation.

I have said that during the first stage of the biblical tradition on marriage the concern was to stress its creaturely character against attempts to give it a false, idolatrous sacredness. The second stage began to highlight its function as a sacred symbol. Marriage was now seen as representing the covenant between God and his people. It stood for the fidelity of God, his steadfast love for his people. This symbolic meaning of marriage was then, in the New Testament, transferred to signify the union between Christ and the Church. Jesus referred to himself as the bridegroom. In the parables he spoke of the coming kingdom as a wedding feast.

The third and final stage in the development of Christian marriage was when marriage was recognized as a sacrament in the full sense, namely as an efficacious sign of grace. Marriage, in itself a secular reality, is seen as becoming, in the context of the life of grace, the presence of the eternal reality of salvation and an active participation in the life of Christ. Marriage remains indeed a worldly reality. In heaven there is no marrying. But it has become a temporal embodiment of eternal life. The intimate closeness of man and wife expresses, embodies, and brings about a closeness to Christ and through Christ to God. The love by which man and wife love each other is the very love by which God loves them and they love God. Their own love for each other is taken up into and transformed by the gift of God's love, granted to them in and through their marital union.

Marriage as a sacrament is not limited to the exchange of consent nor to the first consummation in sexual union, but makes an efficacious sign of grace all during the shared life of the partners including the repeated renewal of their love in sexual intercourse.

The slow recognition of marriage as a sacrament contains a lesson for us. For marriage to be seen as a sacred reality, but in a way that respected the transcendence of God and the sacred, it was first necessary that its secular reality as a permanent and exclusive union of a sexual nature should be firmly established. The concern of Christ was first to restore marriage as a permanent union. Speaking of divorce, he said: "from the beginning it was not so" (Mt 19:8). Today we cannot save Christian marriage simply by proclaiming its sacred character and becoming lyrical about it as a symbol of Christ and the Church. Our first task is to save it as a secular institution. We cannot abandon marriage as a fundamental human reality. The destruction of marriage in our present society is the destruction of Christian marriage, because it removes the very basis of the sacred sign.

What is chiefly destroying marriage in present society is the frequency of divorce. As I mentioned previously, one in two marriages in the United States ends in divorce, and one in three in Great Britain. This is in effect the removal of the institution of marriage from society, with the disintegration of the meaning of sexual intercourse.

Sex is body language. Like all language it can be used in various ways with a variety of meanings. Offhand we can distinguish athletic sex, recreational sex, therapeutic sex, courtship sex, perverted sex, and no doubt one could easily add other modes of sexual expression. Society, let us admit it, has never and will never control all these sexual manifestations. They can, however, be regarded like slang or jargon in ordinary verbal language. They can be tolerated as marginal deviations provided the central language itself remains firm. But there is cause for alarm if the central tradition of the language itself becomes swamped, so that there is only slang and no standard language. Marital sex is the central bodily sexual language. For its development and preservation it demands the context of permanent fidelity through all the vicissitudes of life. Only in such a context can sexual language find its full richness, with its full range of expression from the playful to the sublime. Without fidelity and permanence, sex remains crude and lacks the subtlety that makes its choice as a sacred sign appropriate.

The overwhelming of sexual language by sexual slang has been made possible by easy divorce. That, rather than mere sexual irregularity, is the fundamental disorder of present society, although the two are related, sexual irregularity leading to divorce.

For some reason, Christians always tend to work to solve the last problem but one. At present they are busily proclaiming the goodness of sex and the body. Few people now need convincing of that, though, admittedly, a denial or hatred of sexuality is hidden within much sexual indulgence. All the same, a more pressing problem is to re-establish the reality of marriage as a permanent and exclusive union, within which the sexual nature of human beings can find its full development and expression. Is it not a scandal that there is no difference between the divorce figures for Christians and those for people without Christian faith? How far is this from the Christian ideal? ''For this reason a man shall leave his father and mother and be joined to his wife, and the two shall become one flesh. This mystery is a profound one and I am saying that it refers to Christ and the church'' (Eph 5:31-2).

The Salt of the Earth

"You are the salt of the earth," said Christ to his disciples; "you are the light of the world," he further added (Mt 5:13–14). Is it not ridiculously arrogant to think of ourselves as the salt of the earth and the light of the world? How can we measure the full meaning of that claim made for us by Christ? Let us consider the society to which we have to give a savour, the world which we have to enlighten.

Our society, together with the world to which it belongs, is not Christian. I am not, in saying this, counting the numbers who go to church. That is not a reliable criterion. What I have in mind is the dynamic, the driving force, behind what is happening. I am saying that what is going forward in the world today is not Christian. We are watching a process, the unfolding of purposes that are not in accord with Christian values.

Conservative Christians are only too ready to point to certain symptoms as indicative of a departure from Christian norms: abortion, sexual promiscuity, divorce, pornography, euthanasia. The list is one-sided in its emphasis and too limited in its range. More important to point to the various forms of greed and injustice, to poverty and unemployment, to torture and oppression, to the arms race, to the destruction of the environment for short-term gains. Our society can hardly be described in traditional Christian terms as a faithful people serving God with a quiet mind. What is the dynamic that is causing the restless destructiveness of our present world?

The attempt to answer the question has preoccupied a variety of commentators and thinkers. I must be content here to make a few more obvious comments as a context for a reminder of Christian values.

What we are seeing is the result of a society in which all material business is governed by profit, not by the common good. It is not a question of trying to exclude self-interest, which will always have a prominent place in the work of this world. But what we are experiencing is the swamping of any consideration other than that of financial profit. The question is always and solely what will sell, not what is useful or valuable. Everything is measured in terms of money. In the long term, no one gains from the creation of poverty and the destruction of the environment. But in the short term, some people can gain enormously in material prosperity by ignoring the welfare of others, and dismissing any concern for future generations. Our society is being directed by those who are prepared to sacrifice everything for short-term gains, and many others follow their example for fear of being left behind in the struggle for a comfortable survival. Not many Christians have been able to resist the temptation to follow suit, despite the conflict with their Christian profession.

The other motivation in our society is the will to power. Since the seventeenth century the West, now followed by the rest of the world, has been engaged in a scramble for power. Knowledge is conceived as power. It is a means of control. Calculation is exalted above contemplation, manipulation above receptivity. Reason no longer means a tension or openness towards a reality greater than the self, but the bringing of reality into a subordination to the self, so that it can serve the purposes of the self. Reason becomes the creation of routines through which the whole of reality takes the form of a huge machine under the direction of the autonomous self. We are caught in a mechanical view of reality, in a delusion of the almighty power of the controlling self and in a myth of progress.

But what has all this to do with the average Sunday congregation? How many, if any at all, in our church congregations have any part in determining the direction of our society? We may truly apply to ourselves today what Paul said of the Christians at Corinth: "For consider your call, brethen; not many of you were wise according to worldly standards, not many were powerful, not many were of noble birth; but God chose what is foolish in the world to shame the wise, God chose what is weak in the world to shame the strong, God chose what is low and despised in the world, even things that are not, to bring to nothing things that are, so that no human being might boast in the presence of God" (I Cor 1:26–9). But, notice Paul is not saying that we Christians do not have an important part to play in determining the course of this world. We do; and he is telling us not to be deceived by appearances into forgetting we are indeed instruments of the divine purpose. How, then, can we conceive our impact upon our society and the world?

The key to understanding here is the disproportion that always exists between the trivial appearance and the spiritual reality of good and evil.

Evil cloaks itself in triviality; its appearance is banal. It is seemingly decent people who make the evil decisions that result in oppression and injustice, in exploitation, torture and war, in genocide and mass murder. To see evil as visibly diabolical, as being the work of easily recognizable villains, is to retain a child's view. The real evil in our society is perpetrated by respectable citizens who have successfully smothered their own consciences and beguiled others into accepting their behaviour as merely "realistic."

The slaughter of six million Jews in Hitler's Europe with the co-operation of many "decent" people has made us aware of the contrast that may exist between trivial appearance and the hidden enormity of spiritual evil. But take a lesser example that is, unfortunately, an everyday occurrence — drunk driving. We are prepared to allow that a "decent" person may for the sake of a minor, transitory pleasure seriously risk slaughtering others or permanently disfiguring or crippling them. The figures show that we treat as trivial an action that is a gross evil, the enormity of which we seem to realize only when actually confronted with, say, a mother bewailing the mangled body of her child.

The good is also frequently trivial in appearance. Paul lays down the principle that only the spiritual person can understand the thoughts and gifts of God. "So also," he writes, "no one comprehends the thoughts of God except the Spirit of God. Now we have received not the spirit of the world, but the Spirit which is from God, that we might understand the gifts bestowed on us by God" (I Cor 2:11–12). Again, "The unspiritual man does not receive the gifts of the Spirit of God, for they are folly to him, and he is not able to understand them because they are spiritually discerned" (I Cor 2:14). But it is perhaps a phrase of Isaiah that brings home to us the way in which immeasurable spiritual good may be hidden in seemingly trivial action. Urging us to a spiritual fast which would consist in sharing our bread with the hungry, in bringing the homeless into our house and clothing the naked, Isaiah goes on to say, "Then shall your light break forth like the dawn" (Is 58:8). "Like the dawn" — to do these corporal works of mercy is the dawn of a new age, the manifestation of the Spirit of God.

An exaggeration? Can a few charitable deeds be the dawn of a new age? Let us admit they can be only a salve to our conscience in the context of a life of self-interest. But they can also be the stopping in ourselves of the whole dynamic of our present society. Visibly trivial, those actions can be the manifestation of a refusal to be governed by the pursuit of money and the sign of a denial that the individual self is autonomous and essentially unrelated to others. It is by no means a trivial matter, but it requires the power of the Spirit of God to bring to a halt the dynamism of society in each of our lives.

Certainly, as radical reformers and revolutionaries truly point out, it is not enough for individuals to be personally converted, the institutions of society must be changed. Nevertheless institutions are not changed overnight, nor is it enough simply to destroy what exists. The direction of society must be turned around, and this must be done in people, in the attitudes and actions of human persons. Actions that seem to be trivial may be heavy with the weight of a new force. If Sunday congregations throughout the world lived by Christian values and not by the values of this world, it would indeed be the dawn of a new age.

Despite its horror, the Crucifixion in the political and social context of the time was a trivial incident. Thousands under the Roman power had been crucified. It was not, however, spiritually trivial, as its subsequent transformation of the Roman world clearly showed, because it was in effect a rejection of the value-system of the time. Jesus challenged the contemporary society, and that is why he was put to death. One could say that the message of the Crucifixion is that if you genuinely live according to the values of Christ, the world will put you to death. Try living the Christian life without compromise and see then whether what is asked of you is trivial. Jesus brushed history against the grain; our task is to do the same in our contemporary context.

We cannot avoid sharing the experience of our society to some extent. That experience is the experience of the absence of God. The feeling of absence is a result of the breakdown of traditional symbolism and the pressure of an autonomous self, seeking freedom from traditional religious authority. But instead of that sense of absence being experienced in a merely negative way, it can be transformed into a sense of transcendence. But to do that, we must live in our daily lives by a set of values different from those of our fellow citizens, rejecting the pursuit of money and the desire for power. Isaiah tells us that if we do so, "Then you shall call, and the Lord will answer; you shall cry, and he will say, 'Here I am'" (Is 58:9).

Asking for Things

Does it make sense to ask God for things? To pray to God for something we need or for the successful outcome of some enterprise we have undertaken? Or is the prayer of petition, as it is called, an obsolete form of religious practice? The brief answer is to point to the Our Father as the model for Christian prayer. Its petition for daily bread clearly represents all petitions for the fulfilment of our legitimate needs. The rest of the gospel supports that meaning, with its parable of the importunate friend (Lk 11:5-8), followed by the statement of Christ: "Ask, and it will be given you; seek and you will find; knock, and it will be opened to you. For every one who asks receives, and he who seeks finds, and to him who knocks it will be opened" (Lk 11:9-10).

All the same, to pray for things is a practice with which many Christians today are uncomfortable. We live in a scientific age. Science is the reliable knowledge we have of the laws that govern the world. The world, as they say, has become disenchanted, which means we no longer see it as an arena for the activity of spiritual forces. We no longer think, for example, of a guardian angel protecting each of us, both from falling into temptation and from meeting with an accident. We have left behind the poetry of religion and live now in the prose of science. Thunder is not for us the anger of God, but a release of electricity. Where can we find the conviction to ask God for the relief of sickness, for success in examinations, and for the fulfilment of all our other needs. We turn instead to known earthly causes to achieve earthly effects.

There are indeed spiritual effects. We still pray to God to forgive us our sins, to make us holy, to help us to keep the moral law, to be kind, loving, generous, and so on. But most of us would feel embarrassed if called upon to ask God or his saints for good weather, to assist us to get out of financial difficulty, to find us a house, or even to give us physical health. And yet not to do so would seem to be a lack of faith. Should we or should we not ask God for material things, for the good things of this world?

God is an ineffable mystery. We cannot with our human minds apprehend the infinite reality of God. As Thomas Aquinas said, we know that God is, but not what he is. We do not grasp the essence of God. We know him only indirectly through analogies and symbols. This remains true even after the coming of Jesus Christ. The Incarnation itself is a mystery beyond our understanding. If the reality of God as he is in himself is beyond our human understanding, we still have no other recourse but to relate to God in a human way. If God is to enter our lives, we must communicate with him in a human fashion. We talk to God we tell him our needs, we express to him our hopes, we pour out our complaints and our fears. The alternative is to live without the consciousness of God.

No doubt there are times when all that we should do is to remain in silent adoration before the mystery of Godhead, emptying our minds of all concepts, images, words, as utterly inadequate to express the Divine Reality. But even mystics nourish their sense of God by returning from the darkness and silence of mystical union to words and images. For those who are not mystics, to refuse to talk to God in a human manner is to forget his presence. Our consciousness is like a polyphony. There are many voices, all giving utterance simultaneously. Listening to a polyphony, one can easily fail to notice one of the less prominent of those voices. Our attention is absorbed by the more obvious parts. Likewise, in our everyday consciousness, faith or the awareness of the presence of God is a voice that can easily remain unnoticed because our attention is captured by the loud voices of our immediate concerns. To bring God into those concerns by talking to him about them and asking for his help is to ensure that the sense of the presence of God remains vivid and is constantly heard in the somewhat noisy polyphony of our consciousness.

But does not that still leave asking for things a form of make-believe? Apart from giving us a subjective sense of God, does the prayer of petition make any difference to what happens? It can't possibly make any difference in a universe we know to be governed by scientific laws. That objection rests upon a misunderstanding. It is wrong to suppose that the acceptance of science means that everything must be regarded as completely determined, so that to ask for an intervention of God is to call for a miracle. A particular event may fully correspond to all relevant scientific laws, and yet the convergence and combination of factors in that particular instance will leave it contingent or unnecessary, so that it need not have happened, and render it essentially unpredictable. Scientific laws are always hypothetical in relation to particular events. They tell what will happen if certain conditions are fulfilled. Even in the laboratory, those conditions are not always fulfilled. An element of unpredictability is present in the most controlled experiment.

For that reason, the intervention of our free decisions in the order of reality does not presuppose any violation of scientific laws. Scientists, by their free decisions, intervene in the order of nature in the attempt, not always successful, to control particular events. They are helped by their knowledge of scientific laws, but they have as well to manipulate the unique combination of factors that will bring about the particular event they want. In everyday life our use of technology presupposes both the universal validity of scientific laws and our ability to intervene through free decisions in the concrete course of events. It is no contradiction of scientific knowledge to believe that God in his providence freely governs the whole contingent course of events of this universe and in doing so takes account of our prayers. For him to do so implies no violation of any scientific law. There is the difficulty of God's knowledge of our future free acts, but that difficulty is there whether one believes in the prayer of petition or not. The belief in the prayer of petition does not make it any greater.

Science and belief in the providence of God do not clash; they belong to two different orders of explanation. There is a story told of an anthropologist doing field-work in a tribe. A man had been killed by a rock falling from an overhanging cliff. The tribesmen explained his death as a punishment for a ritual violation the man had been guilty of commiting the previous day. The anthropologist pointed out that the cliff was dangerous and that there had been several recent falls of rock. Their response was to say that the frequent rock falls did not explain why the rock fell when that particular person was underneath the cliff. The scientific question is answered by general laws. The religious question is concerned with the particularity of the individual event. Medical science tells us a given disease is caused by a virus. Religion has to cope with the lament, Why me?

Science, then, does not exclude belief in the prayer of petition as making a difference to the actual course of events. The difficulty people find with it cannot be attributed, at least not directly, to science, but to the concept of God it presupposes. Can we really suppose that the Ultimate Reality of the universe is going to help us find the money for a new car?

Now, undoubtedly, the practice of the prayer of petition can be carried out in a childish, ridiculous, unworthy fashion. We have to follow a middle road between the two extremes of childish sentimentality and an inhuman, arrrogant stiffness. We have to communicate with God in a human fashion. As I have already said, we have no alternative. To refuse human talk with God on the grounds of its unworthiness of the divinity is to cloak our own arrogance in a false concern for respect to the Deity. The Bible does not support such stiffness. We should be not childish, but childlike. At the same time, we should recognize that one of the purposes of the practice of the prayer of petition is to educate our desires.

It is good that we should feel that the expression of some desires is unworthy of prayer to God. But that is because to foster such desires is unworthy. We should be embarrassed about praying to win a lot of money, because we should be embarrassed about desiring money in that way. The prayer of petition should serve as an ascetic discipline, purifying our desires and drawing us gradually into God's design of love. As we enter more deeply into the love of God, our prayer will grow. We should allow our prayer to alter, though without forcing the pace. The people who remain childish are those who do not honestly display their desires before God, submittimg them to the divine will. Let us be honest with ourselves in prayer. It is right that a young person should pray for success in a career or for fulfilment in a marriage. An older person after not making it careerwise or after a marriage break-up will be led to a sense of the deeper dimension of God's plan for human beings. Christ's prayer in the Garden, ''nevertheless not my will, but thine be done'' (Lk 22:42), marks the point at which every prayer of petition must eventually arrive. At the same time, many will have to travel a long road before reaching that point, and the prayer of petition should accompany them all the way.

To ask God for things is to submit our desires to God's judgement. It is to accept the frequently painful purification and education of those desires. The reason why such discipline is necessary is to bring our desires into harmony with God's promises. We know not what to ask because God's promises exceed all that we can humanly desire. As Paul tells us, "But, as it is written, 'What no eye has seen, nor ear heard, nor the heart of man conceived, what God has prepared for those who love him'" (I Cor 2:9). Meanwhile, however, let us not be afraid to open our hearts to God. He will slowly teach us what to desire.

The Mind of Christ Jesus

Most thinking Christians today do not know what to make of the traditional claim made for Jesus, that he is the incarnate Son of God. As traditionally understood, the claim is that the person, Jesus Christ, is one in being with the Father. Jesus is, therefore, a pre-existent divine person, who became man. In the unity of one person, without intermingling or confusion, are both divine and human attributes, so that Jesus is truly God, one with the Father from all eternity, and truly man, one with us from the time of his human conception.

That traditional teaching finds magnificent expression in the hymn to Christ, inserted by Paul into his Epistle to the Philippians. The first part of it runs:

> Have this mind among yourselves which is yours in Christ Jesus, who, though he was in the form of God, did not count equality with God a thing to be grasped, but emptied himself, taking the form of a servant, being born in the likeness of men. (Phil 2:6–7)

The hymn ends with the profession of faith that Jesus is Lord, that is, Jesus is given the divine name.

For several centuries the early Church struggled to find an appropriate formulation of the truth of the Incarnation, and it reached, though not without leaving an unresolved conflict and causing a lasting division, a classical dogmatic statement in the Council of Chalcedon of 451. Today a further struggle is taking place to find a new formulation which will complement rather than replace Chalcedon. Christian thinkers are torn between a metaphysical and a symbolic interpretation. A metaphysical interpretation would follow the example of medieval theology. The difficulty is that it inevitably invokes concepts and principles no longer acceptable to modern thought. Moreover, a metaphysical interpretation would seem to do violence to the general characteristics of religious language as analysed in the science of religion. On the other hand, a symbolic interpretation does not, so it seems, do justice to the traditional claim made for Christ by the Church.

I do not want to enter further into the problem of interpreting and formulating the mystery of the Incarnation. I want, instead, to do two things: first, to set forth the reason why the Church has insisted on affirming that Jesus is God; and, second, to ask how we can best fulfil today the command of Paul to make our own the mind of Christ.

Why has the Church insisted upon the divinity of Jesus, upon the oneness of Jesus in his divine nature with the Father? It is because the Church wishes to affirm as a true statement that God has suffered. Because Jesus is a divine person, one in Godhead with the Father, the sufferings of Jesus were the sufferings of God himself. They were the personal sufferings of the Second Person of the Trinity. Through the Incarnation, God identified himself with suffering humanity. He did not merely look upon the sufferings of humanity with compassion. He did not only relieve those sufferings by his own action and the action of his disciples through the ages. He did not merely promise happiness to those who bore their sufferings with patience. He took those sufferings upon himself. The infinite God made himself vulnerable. He now knows by personal experience what it means to suffer. Short though his life was, Jesus underwent a range of suffering: disappointment, failure, betrayal by friends, fear, physical suffering, seeming abandonment by God the Father, death. We can go to Jesus with the assurance that his personal experience allows him to enter deeply into our lament. If Jesus were truly man, but not truly God, we should have had him a fellow human sufferer to sympathize with us and console us, but God would still have remained distant from our sufferings, knowing them in a divince manner, but not sharing them. Because Jesus is truly God as well as truly man, we can say that our God, the God we worship, knows himself what it is to suffer. The Incarnation is the doctrine of a suffering God.

There is no satisfying theoretical answer to the problem of human suffering. Any considerations put forward, for example the educative value of suffering, collapse into inadequacy when we are confronted in the concrete with the excessive character of actual suffering. Human beings are indeed soft, very soft bodies in a hard, a very hard world. No theorizing is of any real help. What alone enables us to work through suffering, so that it becomes productive not destructive, is the support of others who know suffering from within and whose consolation has not been bought cheaply. Christians have a God who learnt how to suffer the hard way. "For because he himself has suffered and been tempted, he is to help those who are tempted" (Heb 2:18).

Let us turn now to the summons of Paul to make our own the mind of Christ. Two insights are revivifying the life of the Church today.

The first insight has given rise to what is called "liberation theology" which is inspiring and guiding the Church in Latin America. Liberation theology is the working out of the conviction that the Christian message of salvation must be embodied and made effectual in the social and political reality of human history. To isolate that message in a purely religious or spiritual realm is to deprive it of meaning. There has, therefore, been a renewal of social concern, not as an extra, but as an essential expression of the Christian gospel. Now, what has given Latin American liberation theology its most distinctive feature is the first insight I have referred to, which can be formulated as the option for the poor.

The option for the poor does not mean simply that the Church is *for* the poor, with sympathy for the poor and oppressed and with a willingness to help them. The Church is the Church *of* the poor. Normatively, it is the community of the poor and oppressed of this world. The rich are not excluded, but they are marginal if the Church at a given time has found its connatural embodiment and expression. The position of the rich Christian, though a possibility, is always anomalous. The reason is that Christian values are not the values of this world. To follow Christian values and at the same time to be successful in terms of this world may occasionally happen, owing to an unusual combination of circumstances, but it is not to be expected. So, Jesus said: "How hard it is for those who have riches to enter the kingdom of God! For it is easier for a camel to go through the eye of a needle than for a rich man to enter the kingdom of God!'' (Lk 18:24-5). But what can happen and what has frequently happened in history is that the powerful of this world take over the Church. They make the Church their Church, and treat the poor as their clients, coming to the Church for help and benefits, but remaining marginal to its structure and action. The option for the poor restores the balance and insists that the Church belongs to the poor. It is first and foremost the community of the poor, oppressed, and weak of this world.

The second insight is that in our following of Christ we should begin not with beliefs about him, but with doing the truth in love. That last phrase is a translation of a Greek verb, *aletheuein*, formed from the Greek word, *aletheia*, for truth. The verb means both speaking and doing the truth, and so the Bible of Jerusalem translates the phrase as ''If we live by the truth and in love'' (Eph 4:15). The point is that what comes first is not an intellectual assent to propositions about Jesus Christ, but an active sharing through love in the truth that Jesus is as the Son of God. I have already said that we live in a time of questioning concerning the interpretation of the doctrine of Christ. That need not distress us. Any new formulation that makes its way in the Church will be in continuity with the old. Meanwhile, what is demanded of us is clear: to live according to the mind of Christ. If we do that, the truth embodied in our actions will find its appropriate formulation in due time. What, then, shall we do?

First, we should live in the recognition that God is close to us in our struggles, difficulties, and sufferings. God is not at a distance, up there somewhere, looking down upon us with sympathy, but not united to us, whether in distress or joy. God is down here, one with us, having his own experience of suffering to share with us. That God is close to us is not always a welcome message. We are tempted to wallow in our sufferings, to give way to self-pity. The thought of God serves as a reality principle, leading us to acknowledge that the good things of the human condition, the immense and subtle range of human sensitivity, are bound up with suffering. Machines do not suffer, but neither do they feel joy. Jesus has taught us how to suffer, but also how to rejoice. The Incarnation is a summons to us to affirm our humanity, accepting its vulnerability, not hardening our hearts, but opening them in love to the throbs of our fellow human beings and those of God himself.

Second, on the level of political action we should support the option for the poor. According to present demographic trends, it is certain that by the year 2000 over 70 per cent of all Christians will live in the Third World continents of Asia, Africa, and Latin America. The Church is becoming again the Church of the poor. It will be their Church. The "normal" Christian will be one of the poor and oppressed. Now, Christians in the First World can meet this shift in either of two ways. They can resent the change in the centre of gravity of the Christian Church and endeavour to keep control over the Church as an institution. Or they can gracefully yield their position of authority to the people of the Third World, recognizing that their own affluence and worldly power make them marginal in relation to Christ's Church and less able to interpret the message of Jesus to those looking for salvation.

The hymn to Christ in Philippians should guide us here. Whatever may be the privileges we Christians in the First World have enjoyed up till now, the time has now come for us to empty ourselves and make ourselves servants of our suffering brethen in the Third World. If we truly humble ourselves in deed and not just in word, we shall be making our own the mind of Christ.

The Rule of God

I dislike the Feast of Christ the King. It was started in the Catholic Church by Pope Pius XI in 1925, and has since been adopted by Anglicans. As established by Pius XI, it was intended as an assertion of the power of Christ against what the Pope called laicism, which meant the secular forces of this world. Now, I hold no brief for secularism, which as the rejection of the religious dimension of life is both an error and an impoverishment. However, the word "laicism," used to designate it, shows that there has been a confusion between secularism and a healthy opposition to a clericalized Church. The Pope in the encyclical inaugurating the feast goes on to speak of the fullness of legislative, judicial, and executive power found in Jesus Christ, which would seem to be a mistaken attempt to conceive the power of Christ in terms of worldly power. At this point, one can only repeat the words of Christ: "My kingship is not of this world" (Jn 18:36), and recall how a misunderstanding of the power of Christ by the Church has marred Christian history, with its Crusades, its religious wars, its cruel persecutions. All the same, the Feast does contain a kernel of truth, and in such matters it is better to rethink and reinterpret rather than to be entirely negative.

The theme of kingship is central to the message of Jesus. Here is how Mark sums up the teaching of Christ: "The time is fulfilled, and the kingdom of God is at hand; repent, and believe in the gospel" (Mk 1:15). The word "kingdom" here does not mean a territory or realm, whether literal or metaphorical, over which God reigns. It means the active rule of God, the exercise of his kingly power. We look to God as the ultimate force in this universe — a force to judge and to save, to love with tenderness and compassion and yet to condemn those who refuse its loving reign.

In accepting the rule of God, we actively share in it. We are not just passive subjects. Peter in his First Epistle speaks of Christians as "a chosen race, a royal priesthood, a holy nation, God's

own people'' (I Pet 2:9). Jesus Christ became a king by accepting
the rule of God and thus sharing in his dominion. We are invited
to do the same: to make our own the rule of God and in that way
to become a kingly people, a royal priesthood. What does this
mean in practice?

The first and perhaps most difficult lesson is not to trust in
worldly power. We say that we place our trust in God, but as
soon as our well-being is seriously threatened we seize upon
whatever worldly help is at hand, showing little moral scruple
in doing so. The prophets were constantly upbraiding the people
of Israel for failing to trust in God and instead seeking political
and military alliances with one or other of the surrounding
nations, thus endangering the distinctive religion and culture of
Israel as God's own people. Reliance upon worldly power eventually led to the political destruction of the nation because they
could not trust in the Lord. We are the same. The arms race is
a clear sign of our insecurity and failure to trust in God and our
fevered willingness to jettison our Christian values in the name
of national security. And we are headed on a path that leads to
destruction, perhaps this time the destruction of the entire human
race. I am not here advocating pacifism, though I respect it as
a possible option, but, whether pacifists or not, we have to
recognize that the search for an ultimate security through worldly
power is a dangerous delusion. There is no ultimate security outside trust in the active rule of God, and that trust has to spring
from faith and love; it does not rest upon any assurance given
by the powers of this world.

The paradoxical character of God's kingship when it is
manifested in the context of this world is made clear in the relationship that John in his Gospel establishes between the crucifixion and exaltation of Jesus. He puts into the mouth of Jesus
the words: ''and I, when I am lifted up from the earth, will draw
all men to myself'' (Jn 12: 32). It is a play upon the word *hupsoun*,
which combines the meanings of lifting up physically and of
exalting. In the quotation from John, Jesus refers both to his death
by being lifted up physically on the cross and to his exaltation.
The same play upon the word *hupsoun* is found in an earlier
passage: ''So Jesus said, 'When you have lifted up the Son of
man, then you will know that I am he, and that I do nothing on

my own authority but speak thus as the Father taught me' '' (Jn 8:28). In other words, for John's Gospel the death of Christ is identified with his exaltation in glory, his exaltation in glory is identified with his death. The active rule of God, his kingly power is to be found in the midst of what in worldly terms is failure and disaster. Pilate unwittingly proclaimed the truth when he placed over the head of Jesus on the cross: ''This is Jesus the King of the Jews'' (Mt 27:37). What for the world was mockery was simple truth before God.

The rule of God is the opposite to fate. If life is going well, we proclaim our belief in the rule of God and dismiss the thought of fate. But if our life is suddenly shattered, we are seriously tempted to believe we are victims of a blind fate. I suppose it is a natural form of self-protection, but when we are prospering, we all find it difficult to realize that we can easily be overtaken by calamity or disaster. Yet, I myself have only to think of what has happened around me, and I am sure the experience of others is like my own.

A colleague of mine in another university lost his wife and two young children, all killed by a car in front of his own house. A distinguished friend of mine, Bishop John Robinson, was told he had cancer and had six months to live; he has since died. A student of mine received a similar announcement, and the occurrence is so frequent that there are few of us without knowledge of such cases. What about all those — and I have known several — who, despite considerable talents and qualifications face endless unemployment. And so one could continue. There is no need to indulge in wide generalizations about the human condition and about the meaning of history to be strongly tempted to believe that we are at the mercy of blind fate. Most people meet enough shocks in their own personal experience to raise a nagging doubt in their minds whether the world and history are under the active rule of a loving God.

There is no satisfying theoretical theodicy or justification of the ways of God. We do not and cannot know enough to answer the questions we raise. It is also a mistake to attribute to God's will without qualification events that are bound up with the laws of nature or with the results of the evil choices of free human wills. But if by the grace of God, together with our experience of the reality of love, we hold fast to the belief that God's rule and not blind fate governs our life, how can we give practical effect to that belief in our everyday lives, so that we do not wait upon disaster before we give expression to our belief?

One way, which has proved very helpful to many, is to practise de Caussade's teaching on the sacrament of the present moment. Jean Pierre de Caussade was an eighteenth-century French spiritual writer. His chief work, *Abandonment to Divine Providence*, has shown many how to live out their belief in the rule of God. He insists that the coming of the kingdom of God is made manifest in the present. We should not be living in the future, which is not yet a reality. We should not be living in the past, which is no longer a reality. It is the present moment which we have to serve God and experience his loving rule. Every present moment is a sacrament or sacred sign, manifesting and conveying the reality of God as king and saviour. Through each present moment God's grace becomes efficacious in our lives. We should not turn away from the present into the future and back to the past. De Caussade's teaching is an application of the saying of Jesus: "Therefore do not be anxious about tomorrow, for tomorrow will be anxious for itself. Let the day's own trouble be sufficient for the day" (Mt 6:34). To live for the day or day by day need not be an irresponsible attitude. It can be the recognition of our own limits in relation to the all-embracing providence of God. The present moment is a sacrament because God is acting in everything that acts upon us, so that we should respond to all that acts upon us so as to respond to the action of God hidden within it.

One further point should be added. We should be ready for the unexpected. Blind fate is monotonous; it constantly repeats itself. God's rule has the unexpectedness of freedom. The improbable happens. So, too, does what is dismissed as impossible by human calculation.

To be ready for the unexpected is that point of the parable of the five wise and five foolish virgins (Mt 25:1–13). This parable is often misunderstood. The virginity of the ten is not part of its meaning. They are ten unmarried maidens, such as would be called upon to attend the bride and bridegroom in a wedding. The saying tacked on to the end of the parable is misleading. It runs: "Watch therefore, for you know neither the day nor the hour" (Mt 25:13). But the ten wise as well as the ten foolish went to sleep in waiting for the wedding party, so that the meaning of the parable can hardly be that we should remain awake, watching. No, not perpetual vigilance, but preparedness for the unexpected is the message of the parable. We should indeed live in the present, doing what is appropriate to the present moment, even if that is sleep. But while living in the present we should always be ready for whatever may meet us in the future.

There are two ways of living in the present. The first is to live by routine, and consequently to be upset and disoriented whenever we are confronted with the intrusion of the new, the unplanned for, the unscheduled, the unannounced. This is to confine ourselves and our lives within merely human limits. It is a practical denial of the transcendent rule of God. How can the action of God be anything other than what in human terms is the incalculable? The other way of living in the present is to be open to whatever comes, no matter how new and unexpected. This is to open to the Spirit, and to allow the sacrament of the present moment to have its effect in transforming our lives. To live only in the future is to live in the unreality of a dream. To live in the present may be to lock oneself into the existing situation, however unsatisfactory. We should live in the present, but in the present as a moment of grace, opening us to what is new.

I suggest, then, that the Feast of Christ the King should not be the occasion for claiming the whole panonply of earthly power for Christ and for Christians in the name of Christ. What it celebrates is the active rule of God as manifested in imitation of Christ in the ordinary lives of the humble and powerless of this world. We should attribute all that occurs to the rule of God and resist the temptation to invoke blind fate when the calamities endemic to the human condition overtake us. But that is not a prescription for passivity. Each present moment should be embraced as having within it the grace of God for the transformation of our individual lives and of the direction of human history. Thy kingdom come.

Beyond Religion

What many people regard as religion is paganism, and Christian faith has rendered paganism obsolete. For that reason it may be thought of as beyond religion.

I am not saying that paganism is evil. Some of the early Christians did so. They attributed pagan religion to the Devil. That was a mistake. Paganism is not evil, but a religious stage we all have to go through. We should not however get stuck in it. The need to go beyond it is why I call it obsolete. Christianity is the going beyond paganism in human history. Each of us has to reproduce that transition in our own lives.

Nor am I saying that the other great world religions, such as Judaism, Buddhism, and Islam, are pagan. The transition beyond paganism has taken place in them as well as in Christianity. It is true that they incorporate pagan elements within their traditions, but so does historical Christianity. What, then, is paganism, and how do we go beyond it?

When Paul and Barnabas came to Lystra, they worked a miracle there by curing a crippled man. On seeing it, the crowd cried out: "The gods have come down to us in the likeness of men!" (Acts 14:11). They called Barnabas Zeus and Paul Hermes and set about worshipping them. Paul and Barnabas stopped them, crying: "Men, why are you doing this? We also are men, of like nature with you, and bring you good news, that you should turn from these vain things to a living God who made the heaven and the earth and the sea and all that is in them" (Acts 14:15). As this incident shows, paganism does not clearly distinguish the divine reality from this world. God or gods belong to the order of the world. No doubt they are seen as a higher or deeper dimension of the world. Nevertheless, they constitute one total order with the rest of reality. What distinguishes the levels of faith higher than paganism is the explicit differentiation of the experience of the transcendent. Since, as Paul and Barnabas proclaim, God has made everything, he is distinct as transcendent from the universe and from every reality it contains. The transition beyond paganism is achieved by the explicit recognition of the transcendence of Ultimate Reality.

That recognition is, however, more difficult to sustain than is often realized. It demands that we relativize all our concepts and images, all our stories and beliefs, concerning God. All these expressions are finite. They do not remove the mystery of God; none can be regarded as absolute or irreplaceable. The divine term towards which our Christian faith is directed is unknown, except indirectly through metaphors and analogies. We meet God in darkness, not in daylight. Those who parade the certitude of their religious beliefs and insist upon a particular expression of religious faith as an unchanging absolute are religiously still pagans. They want a God they can, as it were, see and grasp. They refuse the experience of nothingness, of emptiness, of darkness, which must precede and accompany faith, if faith is to be a response to the transcendent.

But perhaps the contrast between paganism and the higher levels of faith is more clearly seen in the kind of claims made for ritual or for the structure of the religious community. The Christian writers of the second century, the period when Christianity first entered into debate with the educated public of the Roman Empire, expressed the transcendence of Christian faith in a manner that surprises us today — though the surprise is most instructive.

They proclaimed for example: "We have no temple." In doing so, they were echoing these words of Jeremiah against those who relied upon the externals of religion: "Do not trust in these deceptive words: 'This is the temple of the Lord, the temple of the Lord, the temple of the Lord'" (Jer 7:4). But, more importantly, they were continuing a theme of the New Testament, according to which Christ and the Christian community were the New Temple. A temple is a place of the presence of God, a point of juncture between heaven and earth, and meeting-place of the Infinite and finite. That place is no longer a material building, but the living body of Jesus Christ. As John points out in his Gospel, when Jesus spoke of the temple as being destroyed and raised up again, "he spoke of the temple of his body" (Jn 2:21). Paul speaks of Christians as being joined to Christ in forming a temple:" Christ Jesus himself being the cornerstone, in whom the whole structure is joined together and grows into a holy temple in the Lord; in whom you also are built into it for a dwelling-place of God in the Spirit'' (Eph 2: 20-2).

So, as the early Christian writers argued, Christians do not have a material temple. A Christian church is not a temple. The primary meaning of ''church'' is the assembly of the Christian community. A special building is religiously unnecessary. To identify the place of God's presence with a material building is an obsolete form of religion. The dwelling-place of God, the place where we meet God, is the community as the holy people of God, his living temple. To focus upon the church building, to lavish all our care, money, and concern upon it, is to return to paganism.

The early Christian writers went further and declared, ''We have no altar.'' The time of material altars and of material sacrifices upon them has passed. Jesus is now the altar, the victim, and the priest in the spiritual sacrifice of his death. That is the theme of the Epistle to the Hebrews. It was the offering of himself in love for the salvation of the human race on the cross that is now the one sacrifice, renewed sacramentally in the life of the community and in the Eucharist or community meal.

It is not enough to interpret that as the substitution of one sacrifice by another and to fail to recognize that it is a movement to a higher level of religious expression. In the sense in which pagan religions were centred upon a sacrifical ritual as mediating between God and the people, Christianity has no sacrifice. Instead we have access to God by a loving acceptance of the negativities of life, with its sufferings and death. To live in Christ by opening ourselves to his grace is to make our whole life a sacrifice. To quote Paul's exhortation: ''I appeal to you therefore, brethen, by the mercies of God, to present your bodies as a living sacrifice holy and acceptable to God, which is your spiritual worship'' (Rm 12:1).

In line with that understanding, the Church during the first centuries did not refer to its ministers as priests. In the New Testament all Christians are seen as constituting a new priesthood, ''a holy priesthood, to offer spiritual sacrifices acceptable to God through Jesus Christ'' (I Pet 2:5). Jesus himself in the Epistle to the Hebrews is described as the new high priest. But neither in the New Testament nor for several centuries afterwards are the Christian ministers seen as priests in a special sense as distinct from the laity. The Christian community was a priestly people, but it did not have a special priesthood in the same way as the pagan religions. Then, beginning in the second century, there was a gradual transference of the Old Testament texts on priests to the Christian bishops. But it was only in the sixth century that the ministers of the second rank, the presbyters, were called priests. We need not refuse to follow suit. The priestly vocabulary does express something of the nature and function of the Christian ministry. All the same, we should also be able to say that the Christian religion, unlike paganism, is not centred upon a material sacrifice, with a material altar and a special priesthood.

It is possible to misunderstand the force of the word "material" in this context. The contrast is not with "immaterial," as if what was questionable were the visible and tangible things and actions making up the ritual. No, the contrast is with "spiritual," indicating freedom and unexpectedness, what cannot be manipulated, institutionalized, or controlled, because it comes from the free action of God. "The wind," said Jesus, "blows where it wills, and you hear the sound of it, but you do not know whence it comes or whither it goes; so it is with every one who is born of the Spirit" (Jn 3:8). A spiritual religion is a religion that has freed itself from regarding external practices as essential. Religious practices are all dispensable. That does not mean that we must renounce all religious practices and cultivate a purely mystical form of religion. What it does mean is that the Christian religion does not consist in carrying out any specifically religious actions, but in the purification, redirection, and re-motivation of our ordinary, human, everyday actions, but now transformed by the gift of the Spirit.

We should be careful not to interpret the Incarnation in a pagan fashion as if it confirmed that God was part of the order of this world, so that the centre of reality was in humanity and its world. In John's Gospel we are told that Jesus had to go if we were to receive the Spirit. "Nevertheless," said Jesus, "I tell you the truth: it is to your advantage that I go away, for if I do not go away, the Counselor will not come to you: but if I go I will send him to you" (Jn 16:7). It can be put in this way: the gift of the

Spirit is a decentering. The Spirit dislodges us from being focused upon ourselves and our world. It opens us to the transcendent, leaving us without a centre and without being closed in upon a world.

What I am calling paganism is anthropocentric. It is focused upon the human self and its concerns. Spiritual religion, such as Christian faith, is theocentric. The self surrenders to the Spirit, and thereby participates in the reality and action of God. God, not the self, is now at the centre.

The movement beyond paganism, beyond what many people simply identify with religion, is twofold. First, a clear distinction is made between God and the world. God is no longer confused with the order of the universe or with any part, however exalted, within the universe, but acknowledged as the unknown mystery beyond. Second, all religious practices become dispensable because the presence and action of the transcendent God cannot be tied to any specific finite forms. Just as God is distinguished from the universe, so our response to God is distinguished from any particular set of religious practices.

However, there is a sense in which we all have to go through the pagan stage of religious observance. The people who say that they do not need to go to church but they worship God under the open sky would, if they were honest, have to admit that they never think of God from one year's end to the next. How, too, are we going to make children aware of the religious dimension of life, if they are not brought up within a religious tradition with its specific set of religious beliefs and practices? The institutions and ritual of the visible churches are not the essence of Christian faith, but they are its school. A school is not the whole of life, but it is a necessary preparation for its higher stages. Likewise, we need a school of religion, even though we should not confuse it with the essence of religion itself.

The reason, however, for stressing the transition beyond the pagan stage of religious development is the present situation and the opportunity it offers. Throughout the world a new self-consciousness is struggling to be born — a global, critical, corporate self-consciousness, in which human beings of all races, nations, and cultures come together in communication and partnership, acknowledging the unity that binds them together, despite the persistent plurality of their traditions. This new self-consciousness is economic, political, ethical, concerned with peace and justice, but it is not, save in a marginal way, religious. In so far as it includes an implicit striving of humanity towards transcendence, it is a new paganism. It is not a secularism as excluding transcendence, but it is pagan as not clearly differentiating the transcendent. Christians have to draw out and make explicit the implicit transcendent grounding of the new self-consciousness. They cannot do so if they remain fixated in a pagan fashion upon their past and present religious institutions, beliefs, and practices.

In brief, Christianity will again become a social force if Christians enter into freedom of the Spirit, which brings about the genuinely new and allows us constantly to change, because the Spirit prevents us identifying God with any particular finite order or his worship with any particular set of religious practices.

To Live by the Spirit

The Spirit is the gift Christ came to bring. The Spirit is the gift he sent us when he returned to heaven. That gift relates us to the Father as our origin and end and makes us one with Christ, our mediator and our brother. Their mutal love is the Spirit, who dwells within us and unites us to them both.

What, then, does it mean to live by the Spirit? Since it is traditional to use the number seven, let me give the following enumeration: to live by the Spirit means to live creatively, joyfully, in holiness, peacefully, faithfully, modestly, and in the glory of the Resurrection.

To live creatively: Veni Creator Spiritus. *Come Creator Spirit.*
The Hebrew word translated as "spirit" means both breath and the wind. In both senses it evokes the creative, vivifying action of God. God breathed into creatures the breath of life, so that the flesh might live. The wind coming from the sea brought rain and caused the earth to bring forth vegetation. Hence, using that fact as a symbol we pray: "Send forth thy Spirit and they shall be created and thou shalt renew the face of the earth."

The Spirit, as the divine creative principle, is love. The divine love is creative because it is gratuitous. In other words, the divine love is not measured by the merit of the recipient. God's love is not a response to a prior lovableness on our part, but it makes us lovable. When we share in God's creative love, our love is not limited to people who are already lovable, but our love embraces the unlovable and creates new goodness.

Our world at present is trying to solve all its problems by power and domination, which means by rearranging what already exists. It is uncreative. There is no opening out to new possibilities in human personal and social relationships. Because of that, we are living off the capital left by past generations. To live by the Spirit is, in contrast, to live creatively, never closing off the possibility of something entirely new in one's own life and in the life of society.

To live joyfully Da perenne gaudium.
"Give perpetual joy," as we sing in the *Veni Sancte Spiritus*. Joy is the expansion of our minds and hearts that comes from being rooted in the good. It is the presence of the Spirit that roots us in the good. The overwhelming joy brought by the Spirit is expressed in the early Christian tradition by the theme of spiritual drunkenness. The Acts of the Apostles tells us that when the crowd saw the behaviour of the first Christians at Pentecost at the descent of the Spirit, they said: "They are filled with new wine" (Acts 2:13). The early writers seized upon the remark, describing the ecstatic and overflowing joy given by the Spirit as a kind of drunkenness.

The opposite to joy is sourness of mind and heart. When we are not ourselves rooted in the good, when our relation to the good is uncertain, wavering, insecure, we resent good in others. We find ourselves unable to rejoice. The goodness of others seems like a judgement upon ourselves. When we are steadfast in the good, we experience a deep joy at the goodness of others.

To live in holiness: Come Holy Spirit.
The holy is what is separate, what lies apart. God is holy because he is other; infinitely holy because infinitely other. To be with God, we have to go out of ourselves. We have to become decentred, so that the self is no longer our centre of gravity, no long the focus of our concern. God's self-communication is human self-transcendence.

It is not easy to turn away from the self as centre and surrender ourselves to the reality of God. Teresa of Avila remarked on how many entered the mystical path and how few went beyond the first stages. Her explanation was the fear of self-surrender that held people back. But think of the immense relief we should experience if we could, even for a time, forget ourselves, if we could just plunge ourselves into reality without viewing everything through the narrow angle of the self. That would be to live in holiness.

To live peacefully.
Peace is not just the cessation of hostilities. Peace means fulfilment, plenitude, happiness; in particular, the completion that comes from reconciliation among the divided, the restoration of

wholeness. ''Peace,'' said Jesus, ''I leave with you: my peace I give to you; not as the world gives do I give to you'' (Jn 14:27). The Spirit sent by Christ gives us a new plenitude, and therefore a new peace.

Why do human beings not live in peace? Why is peace so difficult to achieve even among Christians? It is because we place our desires in what cannot bring fulfilment. Hence we are restless. We move from one thing to another. We become victims of insatiable desires. This leads us to see others as rivals. We try to satisfy our desires by possession, by appropriating objects, and we clash with others in pursuing these objects. The peace sent by Christ, which is the plenitude of the Spirit, does not provoke rivalry, but brings reconciliation.

To live faithfully.
Faithfulness is one of the fruits of the Spirit as listed by Paul (Gal 5:22). To be faithful is to remain firm and steadfast in hope even when the going gets rough. Hope differs from both optimism and despair in not knowing the answers. The optimist *knows* that everything is going to be all right. The desperate *know* that everything is going to turn out badly. Hope remains open like a question. The ground for the unshaken expectation is the faithful relationship.

Faithfulness is often seen as dull, as opposed to freedom and creativity. But freedom is the outcome of faithfulness; it does not come first. We have to become free, and that requires fidelity to our ideals, values, and purposes. Likewise, all creativity requires time. To create something worthwhile is a long haul. Mere satisfaction is repetitive, cyclic; fulfilment is a struggle forward. It requires faithfulness.

The presence of the Spirit gives us the courage to be faithful, sustains us in hope, and is the source of a creativity that never flags.

To live modestly.
That means to live in depth. Immodesty is living on the surface. Ours is a very immodest age. It is superficial. It has nothing to uncover. It lets it all hang out. What a contrast with Augustine,

for whom the human heart was an abyss, with hidden, un-sounded depths! It is not on the surface, but in the depths of our being that we meet God. The immodesty of our age, which leaves human beings with nothing below the surface, is undoubtedly one of the reasons why people do not pray as they did. The sexual associations and consequences of immodesty do not exhaust its meaning and importance. It is not the modest who are repressed, but the immodest, because these close off their depths and ad-mit only their surface. It is the Spirit who opens our depths and guides us into all truth.

To live in the glory of the Resurrection.
The word "glory" in John's Gospel is a word that indicates divinity. "And the Word became flesh and dwelt among us, full of grace and truth; we have beheld his glory, glory as of the only Son from the Father" (Jn 1:14). The divinity of Jesus is thought of as a radiance, as a glow of light from the depths of his being.

The painter Van Gogh wanted to paint ordinary objects and persons so that they had a glow, like that given by the traditional halo. He succeeded in doing so. In his paintings a pair of shoes, a chair, a vase of sunflowers glows with an intensity that opens our minds and hearts to the depths of the divine reality that sur-rounds and penetrates all finite reality: "In him we live and move and have our being" (Acts 17:28).

To live in the glory of the Resurrection is to allow ourselves to be irradiated through the Spirit with the divine life. But the radiance must come from the depths. The gift of the Spirit makes us already share the risen life of Christ, which penetrates and transfigures the ordinary events of our everyday lives. But the radiance coming from the Spirit is quiet and soft and gentle. To experience it we have to turn off the bright lights of the world, and turn down its harsh noise. If we do so, not merely we, but the world and other people, will become radiant with the glory promised in Isaiah:

> And the glory of the Lord shall be revealed,
> and all flesh shall see it together,
> for the mouth of the Lord has spoken. (Is 40:5)

Christian Hope in a Nuclear Age*

It has become commonplace in Christian thinking over the last decades to hold that Christian hope is for the fulfilment of history. There was a reaction against the other-worldly and individualistic conception, according to which our hope as Christians was for each of us to enter the happiness of heaven in the next world as a reward for our virtuous endurance in this vale of tears. In contrast, it has been stressed, our hope is grounded upon faith in God as the Lord of history, who has acted and still acts in history for our salvation. The Bible has been read as *Heilsgeschichte* or saving history, namely, as a narrative of God's mighty acts in history to achieve his purposes and defeat his enemies.

From that perspective, Jesus Christ is seen as the definitive saving act of God. He is both the centre and the end of human history. He is the centre, because he completes all that has gone before and anticipates all that is to come. He is the end, because in him we find already present all the reality and power that will bring history to its fulfilment. In that sense, history has an eschatological meaning; it is the movement of humanity towards the kingdom of God as the final end of God's creation.

Admittedly, theologians are not in agreement concerning the relationship between eschatology and history, namely between the final kingdom and the presence of God's salvation in history. For some, the final kingdom lies in the future; it is still to come, and its coming will coincide with the end of history. For others, the final kingdom is already realized within history, present in a hidden fashion and still to be made manifest, but present all the same in its saving reality. There are also those who attempt a compromise: the final kingdom is present indeed in its reality,

*The fourteenth Robinson T. Orr Lecture, Huron College, London, Ontario, March 1984.

not just proclaimed as future, but in an anticipatory presence, so that we still await the fullness of its presence and power, its full accomplishment, which we shall experience as the fulfilment of our hope at the end of history. But common to all these interpretations of the final kingdom is the affirmation that human history does have a meaning and purpose, and is intrinsically related to the plan of God as Lord of history to bring about the kingdom as the fulfilment of his promise of salvation.

Is that vision of history as the working out of God's plan of salvation compatible with the expectation that the human species is going to be annihilated by an all-out nuclear war? If not in its present form, can it be modified so as to leave intact the substance of our hope?

At the outset, it should be stressed that the expectation that the human species will be annihilated in the not-too-distant future is not an exaggerated fear, but a calm, sober estimate of the factors operative in the present situation.

There are, first, the probable effects of a full-scale nuclear war. Here we must dismiss the deceptive assurances of political spokesmen. For example, as reported in *Maclean's*,[1] Thomas K. Jones, U.S. deputy undersecretary of defence, predicted a survival rate of eighty percent and a full recovery of the United States within four years after a nuclear war. *Maclean's* recorded that fatuous statement in the context of an account of a meeting of scientists in Washington in November 1983, who under the heading "The World after Nuclear War" set forth the results of two years of studies on the effects of an all-out nuclear war. Their findings showed that any forecast of a substantial survival rate was pure fantasy. The long-term effects might well leave no human survivors in the Northern Hemisphere, and the extinction of the human race could not be excluded as a possibility. I will not outline the frightful details of how such total destruction would be brought about. Many of us are familiar with the vivid account in Jonathan Schell's *The Fate of the Earth*.[2] The point I wish to make here is that we have to envisage, not as a fantasy, but as a real possibility embedded in the present situation, that the human species will be shortly annihilated or reduced to tiny groups of injured and half-crazed survivors, with the cessation thus of human history. No one knows the exact effects of a nuclear war because these have to be hypothetically deduced and cannot be experimentally verified, but scientists would generally maintain that our ignorance is more likely to lead us to underestimate than to overestimate the long-term effects. The global disturbance would be so vast that the consequences are incalculable.

In the light of that sober assessment, we must reject what might seem an attractive approach to the interpretation of imminent nuclear destruction. This would be through an adaptation of the apocalyptic vision of renewal through destruction. The apocalyptic writers lived in a time of oppression and persecution, when seemingly no hope could be placed in political solutions. They looked instead for a divine intervention to bring about deliverance. That divine intervention would be a judgement, destroying the present world order and the wicked with it and a saving act, transforming the face of the earth, renewing it for the righteous. The structure of apocalyptic thinking is, then, to see the new as arising from the ashes of the old, a new world, a new earth coming from the destruction of the existing world. It is tempting to try to apply that mode of thinking to the present situation of political impasse and nuclear threat.

The human species certainly seems to be caught in a political position with no exit. There are no signs of the higher wisdom, the combination of openness and prudence, of boldness and caution, required to lead us beyond the present policy of relying upon a balance of terror to keep the peace. Understandable, therefore, that some people, unable to bear the present tension, are seduced into accepting that nuclear war is to come, but see it as an apocalyptic destruction, renewing the face of the earth, a process of purification, allowing us to begin again, a cancellation of all our present political problems and the entry into a new era. A naive version is that America would survive and be then free to build a new world order. Others cherish a science-fiction version, in which a small surviving group begin human history over again. A religious version would interpret nuclear annihilation as Armageddon, ushering in the Second Coming and the inauguration of the final kingdom.

The response to these attempted interpretations is to repeat that an all-out nuclear war excludes any meaningful survival. Even were considerable numbers to survive in the Southern Hemisphere conditions on this planet would be such as to render impossible any continuation or recuperation of the process of human history. The people would indeed be survivors, hanging on for a limited period to what remained of the environment required for human living. As for the religious version, I think we must rethink our use of apocalyptic symbols. That renewal or transformation may come through destruction or violence is true only in a limited context; it is certainly not true of nuclear destruction. Nuclear annihilation may, I suppose, be taken as God's judgement in the sense that the consequences of human folly may be seen as God's judgement. But to me it is sheer blasphemy to think that the senseless destruction of this beautiful earth has any intrinsic link with the final kingdom or is intended by God as its inauguration.

Granted the irreparable destruction that would be caused by a nuclear war, the second set of factors in determining the present situation concerns the degree of likelihood of the occurrence of an all-out nuclear war. Some might want to argue that, because a full-scale nuclear war would annihilate the aggressors as well as the defenders, so that there can be no winning side, no one would be so foolish as to start such a war. The very destructiveness of nuclear weapons, it is argued, precludes their use, provided both sides possess them. The policy of deterrence will continue to ensure peace.

To leave aside the possibility of the setting into motion of a nuclear exchange by an error and the sterility of a policy of mere deterrence, the argument does not take account of the social and political dynamic that E.P. Thompson calls "exterminism."[3] His general point is that wars do not take place through the conscious planning and decision of a ruling few. Were that so, we might sleep in peace, because the ruling elites would not be likely to plan and decide upon their own destruction. But wars do not usually occur in that way. They come as the final, often unforeseen, outcome of a dynamic created in society by the cumulative impact of many lesser policy decisions, a dynamic leading the society with ever-increasing momentum towards war. When war actually breaks out, it is impossible to assign a particular cause or blame the decision of a particular individual. Thus, through a host of political and economic policy decisions, there is developing in the superpowers a dynamic towards nuclear war. The production of nuclear weapons, for example, has its ramifications throughout the economy. It is a built-in part of the present economic order, so that the cessation of their production would cause an economic crisis. The political movement towards nuclear war may be verified by examining what has happened politically since the end of the Second World War. No one can deny that we have moved inexorably through a multitude of political decisions towards a final conflagration. Hence "exterminism," which Thompson coins by analogy with "militarism" or "imperialism" and which he defines as "these characteristics of a society — expressed, in differing degrees, within its economy, its polity and its ideology — which thrust it in a direction whose outcome must be the extermination of multitudes."[4]

My purpose here is to establish the actual context in contemporary reality for Christian hope. Christian hope would be nothing but an illusion were it to depend upon an untrue assessment of the real state of affairs. Hence my insistence that we are living under the shadow of the strong likelihood that before long the human species will be exterminated in the irrational, purposeless self-destruction of a nuclear exchange. My insistence should not be taken as any gloating over imminent disaster. I wish to God that I and my children did not have to live with this threat, but I cannot continue to hope by hiding from its reality.

Christians, it seems to me, are in a similar position to that of the Jews after the Holocaust. The Holocaust, the slaughter of six million Jews and the sustained, almost successful attempt to annihilate the Jewish race, left Jewish thinkers asking how they could reconcile their traditional belief in God as Lord of history with such an enormity. How could the blank horror of that event, empty of all human feeling or value, be brought under God's providential ordering of history, either as a judgement or as a deliverance? Richard Rubenstein caused some stir by arguing that the Holocaust had made the traditional conception of the God of history untenable,[5] but even those who kept their ancestral faith in God's love for his chosen people had to rethink its implications. Christians now have a parallel task. If we push aside science-fiction fantasies on the one hand and the comforting lies of politicians on the other, the threat of nuclear war confronts us with the prospect of a blank horror of the immediate death of millions, of the frightful suffering of millions more and of the senseless destruction of the entire achievement of centuries of human endeavour. How can any religious faith make that meaningful? How can we dare still speak of Christian hope?

Well, we should begin by acknowledging what Christian hope does not tell us. It does not tell us that nuclear annihilation will not happen. Christian hope does not give us any assurance that the human species will survive the nuclear threat. It does not carry with it any certitude that God will prevent the worst happening, so that somehow or other under God's providential guiding of history a solution will be found that allows history to continue.

The truth is we do not know God's plan for this vast universe. Why do we suppose that the human species is at the centre? Within the context of the universe as a whole, the human species with its history may well prove to be an unsuccessful experiment. Acceptance of the scientific theory of evolution has made us aware that God has created a universe in which one partial order succeeds another through a process of trial and error. The human species, like the dinosaurs, may be destined to disappear in favour of other, more successful, intelligent species.

To shake ourselves free from the remnants of a false anthropocentrism, let us briefly consider a recent presentation of ethics from a theocentric perspective by the Christian writer, James Gustafson.[6] Gustafson argues that God's purposes, in so far as they can be discerned, are for the well-being of the whole of creation, not centrally for human beings. Indeed, there are no grounds, he says, for asserting that the purposes of God in the universe always work out for the benefit either of human individuals or of the human species. He contends, instead, for a theocentric perspective that acknowledges that human beings are not the measure of all things, that human salvation is not the chief, let alone the exclusive end of God. We cannot assume a happy coincidence between the divine law and human fulfilment; the law of God does not guarantee benefits to oneself, one's community, or to the human species as a whole. The chief end of human beings themselves is not their own salvation, but to honour, serve, and glorify God.

Now, I find myself unable to accept that version of theocentrism. I fail to see how the gospel message of salvation through Christ retains any meaning if human fulfilment, both of individuals and of the species, is expendable for a wider purpose in God's governance of the universe and not an inviolable because covenanted part of God's purposes. Hence an orientation towards human fulfilment as guaranteed by God is, *pace* Gustafson, a sound ethical attitude. At the same time, we can admit that there are no grounds for identifying human fulfilment as a central purpose of the universe, and not just a partial end, nor does human fulfilment imply the continuance of the human species within this visible universe. Human fulfilment, both individual and collective, transcends the course and the outcome of human history understood as the pattern of human activities within the material universe. Such human fulfilment may well be a partial element in a wider, transcendent order, at present unknown to us in its particularity.

What about the cosmic role attributed to Jesus Christ in Colossians and Ephesians? I think that must be understood in accordance with the presuppositions of the first century A.D. The texts represent a refusal to subordinate Christ to heavenly powers or emanations as imagined by a primitive Gnosticism. They affirm that Christ is no mere intermediate being, but that in him is the very fullness of God. Such a high Christology, formulated before the vastness of this universe was known, does not, however, exclude other incarnations in other intelligent species elsewhere in this universe. Nor does it require us to hold that the Son of God or Logos in his incarnate manifestation as man exercises a headship or saving mission in regard to all the species of this entire universe.

I would not myself want to elaborate such speculations any further. My chief point runs in the opposite direction. It is our lack of knowledge of God's purposes which should prevent us from identifying the meaning of the universe with the survival of the human species within it. Human survival is not, therefore, the ultimate value in the context of the nuclear threat. For a secular humanist, who sees humankind as the sole, autonomous source and ground of all moral values, the extinction of the human species is the onset of meaninglessness and nothingness. In short, it turns humanism into nihilism. For a Christian believer in a transcendent God and transcendent salvation, this is not the case. There is no reason to suppose that the extinction of the human species would frustrate God's wider purposes for this universe, and the human species, though cut off by its own sins and errors from the actualization of its full potential for worldly development, will still participate in those wider purposes and in the transcendent order that constitutes the ultimate end of all creation.

The refusal to regard human survival as the ultimate good is relevant to the discussion of the moral questions raised by nuclear policy. There is an evident absurdity in risking the extinction of the human species for the sake of the particular political and economic goals of some state. But while that is so, it is not absurd to risk human extinction for the sake of higher values, such as justice, peace, and spiritual freedom. It has been widely regarded as a sign of moral nobility to surrender one's life to a higher cause, and if the death of the species is the only way of preserving moral integrity it would seem to be an acceptable cost. The morality of nuclear policy cannot be decided by the principle of survival at any price. The key moral problem, then, is not how to secure human survival. It is whether any higher purpose can ever be served by inflicting or being willing to inflict the violence of nuclear war, with the immeasurable human suffering and unimaginable physical, social, and cultural destruction it would bring, whether on the contrary the willingness and active preparation for waging a nuclear war are not already corrupting our societies, twisting them in inhuman shapes because of waste of human and physical resources and the increasingly tyrannical security measures required. Can a decent, humane society be a society poised to launch a nuclear attack or reprisal?

The pacifist tradition already rejects all use of violence for any desirable human purpose. It sees in nuclear war and the dilemmas it poses simply an extreme example of the moral bankruptcy of any appeal to violence as a means of achieving a morally acceptable end. The just-war tradition, admitting the use of violence, has always insisted on discrimination in that use of violence and the preservation of some proportion between the violence and the end in view. The question is whether of its very nature nuclear war is such as ever to allow the imposition of any limits, so that it would be at all meaningful to speak of discrimination or proportion.[7]

We would seem, therefore, to be locked into a situation in which a large slice of our resources is devoted to the preparation of a war for which there is no moral justification and which, because of its unlimited character, cannot be brought within the framework of any political, economic, or social policy. What locks us into this absurd situation is the genuine fear that without the threat posed by our nuclear weapons we should fall under the domination of Russia. What can we do, short of surrender to a power that denies values we cherish, other than preserve a shaky balance of terror?

If Christian hope does not give us the easy assurance that nuclear annihilation will not happen, neither does it provide a ready answer telling us what we should do in the present complex situation. In other words, hope, with its reliance upon God's promise of salvation to those who do his will, is not a substitute for the difficult task of moral reasoning. To indicate how difficult a task it is, let me refer to a recent essay by Ronald Green, "Moral Axioms for the Nuclear Age."[8] One of his axioms is: "In the realm of nuclear policy, matters are hardly ever what they seem." The world of nuclear policy is a topsy-turvy world. To give an example. The policy called MAD, meaning Mutually Assured Destruction, which is based upon the threat of massive counter-city retaliation for any nuclear first strike, is less likely to lead to nuclear war than the deployment of selective, accurate counter-force weapons aimed at enemy bases. The reason is that an accurate counter-force system, capable of disarming the enemy, makes a pre-emptive first strike a tempting choice and creates a strong fear of such a strike on the part of the enemy. Hence each side is in the position of having to launch its missiles at the slightest sign that the other side has launched its — indeed, even before. In an international crisis, each side will have a finger hovering over the button, fearfully trying to anticipate a disarming first strike on the part of the opponent. The most dangerous feature in the present situation is the destabilizing effect of the development and deployment of accurate counter-force weapons. Which, then, is the morally responsible policy — to threaten the blanket destruction of centres of population in retaliation for any

nuclear attack, a policy which has proved to be an effective deter-
rent, or to establish an accurate counter-force system, capable of
destroying the bulk of one's opponent's missiles, a policy which
seems more discriminating, but which greatly increases the
likelihood of nuclear war?

It is not my intention here to enter further into the moral debates
concerning nuclear warfare. My concern is with the object and
structure of Christian hope in the context of our present situation. What can we hope for? What form will our Christian hope
take in this nuclear age? So far I have argued that Christian hope
does not give us any assurance that nuclear annihilation will not
occur nor does it give us any snap answers to the moral dilemmas
we face. What, then, is its contribution?

The nuclear threat would seem to have created an un-
precedented situation. Yet, when we reflect upon that situation
in the light of Christian faith, we find it is simply the human condition writ large, the human predicament raised to a new pitch
of intensity or, at any rate, manifested with a new degree of
clarity. Thus, confronted with the nuclear threat, we discover our
moral impotence. We are not capable of the moral awareness or
the moral commitment or the moral achievement required by the
situation. We despair because we cannot save ourselves, because
we see no prospect of bringing ourselves, the members of our
own society or those of other societies to the level of moral self-
transcendence called for if we are to avoid a nuclear holocaust.
But when have Christians ever believed in self-salvation? What
have we in our nuclear impasse but the power of sin and the need
for grace, which have been the perennial content of the Christian message? For Christian hope to come on the scene as meaningful, we must acknowledge our moral bankruptcy, the depths
of our spiritual disorder or, in traditional language, our sinfulness.
Christian hope meets our despair or, alternatively, our presump-
tion — even in our present predicament, there are those whose
groundless self-confidence is irrepressible — by turning to God's
promise of rescue or salvation, as embodied for Christians in Jesus
Christ. But what exactly has God promised? To answer that is
to learn what we may legitimately hope for.

God's promise is not simply a promise of an other-worldly
salvation. It is a distortion of God's promise, made clear as such

by biblical teaching, to relegate salvation to another world or to the future. We already have and experience the reality of salvation. That reality is dynamic, and we still await its full unfolding and manifestation, its full achievement or effects. That fulfilment cannot be enclosed within the narrow confines of society and politics or of the course of history as we know it this side of death. The kingdom, which is what God has promised, is a new community, embracing the dead as well as the living, transcending therefore space and time. But it is already present here and now, existing in, with, and under the social and political order characteristic of human life this side of death. The kingdom of God is already amongst us.

To put it in another way. Human life is lived simultaneously on several different levels, related hierarchically, so that each further level is a higher integration, subsuming the activities of the lower levels. Thus, human intelligence in the concrete is a higher integration of human living, subsuming human biological and sensory activity. The new life of grace or salvation or life within the kingdom is, under various designations, a higher integration of human living, taking up unto itself all the lower levels of human existence and activity.

The new and higher integration of human living, which is the life of grace, is not just an individual affair. It is a new communion among human beings, binding them in a higher fashion to one another as well as to God. This new communion is not a substitute for social and political activity, any more than human intelligence is a substitute for human biological life; the new communion is a higher integration of social and political activity. Since, however, participation in the new communion requires a response to God's grace and is blocked by sin or the refusal of that grace, social and political activity are only very partially integrated into the new communion and are largely marked by the disintegration or disorder of sin. Nevertheless, those who do respond to God's grace should be led, not to withdraw from social and political activity, but to strive to bring that activity under the higher integration of the kingdom. It is a distortion to interpret the kingdom or new communion of grace as existing only on the level of the individual or as existing without any relationship to the social and political order. Here, however, we meet another negative factor in human existence which renders human history an enigma, namely, death. Along with sin, death prevents one interpreting either individual human existence or human history as the smooth, uninterrupted unfolding of an immanent purpose. Take individual death. It is not just a transition but a destruction. Belief in personal survival, whether expressed as the resurrection of the body or the immortality of the soul, does not mean the replacement of life in this world by an entirely new and different life in the next world. That would deprive this life of any intrinsic meaning. The overcoming of death means that there is a level or levels of human existence here and now that are not and cannot be destroyed by death. We already enjoy eternal life. The higher integration of human activity we call grace or union with God passes through death and continues beyond death into new conditions of existence, though remaining essentially the same life. The question of immortality is, Are we already living the kind of life that will be unaffected by death? If our life is, for example, totally absorbed in making money, there is nothing that can meaningfully survive death. Death is thus a transition of life eternal from one state to another. But death is not just a transition. It comes most frequently, as far as our human vision can see, inopportunely — like a thief in the night. We cannot take it as the norm that death comes when a person is ripe in years, with work completed and the character rounded into maturity. More often than not, death cuts a person off with work and character unfinished, so that death takes on the visage of a senseless destruction. As far as individuals are concerned, we have to admit that we cannot relate life before death and life after death together, so as to form a meaningful pattern or shape. Hence we oscillate between so stressing the life to come that this life loses its meaning and value and so stressing this life with its manifold concerns that we cannot make sense of a life beyond death. We do not, then, have knowledge of the shape of our individual destiny. It is hope that steps in where knowledge fails.

Similar considerations apply to the new life of grace as a new community, subsuming social and political activity as a higher integration. It straddles death. There is a level of community that is not affected by death. At the same time, to our limited vision, there is no clear intelligible relationship between the community present here and now as an emergent higher integration of human social existence and the community as continuing beyond death and history. Death retains its arbitrariness as a social as well as an individual phenomenon. It is not the case that human history unfolds towards a particular point and then thus prepared takes a quantum leap into a new order. The dynamism of human history towards the integration of human activities in an achieved social order, worthy of human beings as human and as children of God, is constantly frustrated by the arbitrary incidence of death as well as by sin. From that perspective, the probability that the human species will be exterminated and human history brought to an end in the absurd event of a nuclear war is in line with the absence of intelligible meaning in history generally. We do not know how everything works out or what are the full dimensions of God's plan. We do not know how to relate our efforts to embody the kingdom in the present reality of society and history — essential as those efforts are as a manifestation of our own participation in the kingdom — to what will be the final fulfilment of that kingdom, blocked and cancelled as our efforts constantly are by sin and death. Again, hope must step in where knowledge fails.

Hope, then, is not knowledge of the future, knowledge of how things will work out. Nicholas Lash[9] puts it well when he says that hope is articulated in the interrogative mood. Christian hope, he says, is a question cast as a request — ''Thy Kingdom come.'' He contrasts hope with the twin temptations of optimism and despair. Both optimism and despair agree in claiming to know the answer, though they give opposite answers. Hope makes no such claim. ''Now hope that is seen,'' writes Paul in Romans, ''is not hope. For who hopes for what he sees? But if we hope for what we do not see, we wait for it with patience.''[10] As individuals before our death and as belonging to the human species before it comes to the end of its history, we still stand in the midst of our personal story and the story of our species. The story is as yet open and the outcome not determined, and, as with all genuine stories, we cannot predict the ending; it will surprise us when it comes.

But hope is nearer to despair than it is to optimism. Paul in the quotation I have just given speaks of hope as waiting with patience, and in the traditional theology of hope, the object of hope is a *bonum arduum,* a good the seeking and obtention of which is surrounded by difficulty. Christian hope, according to Lash,[11] is akin to tragic joy, in which through the tragic experience itself desperation is somehow transcended. If I may elaborate that. With Christian hope the tragic experience is transcended without being cancelled or eliminated because in the midst of the tragedy there remains the experience of transcendent love. In an earlier passage in Romans Paul writes: ''and hope does not disappoint us, because God's love has been poured into our hearts through the Holy Spirit which has been given to us.''[12] Hope is grounded upon a faith-experience, in darkness, of the indefinable reality of God's love. In other words, there is a felt and active presence of the reality of the kingdom, manifesting itself in us as a self-transcendent love, moving us beyond our self-interest, creating in us an unrestricted openness that is not emptiness but a relationship to mystery, giving us a strength and endurance, a confidence and assurance, which cannot be either supported or destroyed by any finite event or reality. Hence the tragic joy when such love, assurance, and power are experienced in the midst of disaster.

What, then, is the contribution of Christian hope in the context of the threat of nuclear annihilation? Not to give us knowledge of the outcome. Its contribution rather lies in its refusal to despair, its ceaseless activity to deflect humankind away from its present course which will end in self-extermination, its conviction that the power and reality are already present through which the direction of history can be changed and the human situation transformed. The reality of salvation is already present; it is for us to respond to it. It is never too late to repent and change. That is why Christians will continue to work with quiet confidence in situations which others shrug off as hopeless. To make the point as sharp as possible: until the nuclear button is pressed, those possessing Christian hope will continue to insist that disaster is not inevitable, that there is a real saving potentiality present in the situation, able to transform it and achieve peace and reconciliation. However black the prospect, Christians can never accept that human beings are the helpless, powerless victims of some evil force, whether that is identified with sin or fate or the devil or inherent human weakness. And if and when the nuclear button is pressed and the human species annihilates itself, then hidden in that event will still be the mysterious love of God, even though no one may be left in this world to acknowledge it.

But here I am thrown back, repelled by what I am saying. I share the experience of others who have read a little about the dangers and effects of nuclear war that the thought of the horror it would bring, the unimaginable, unspeakable suffering of millions and the enormity of the destruction of this beautiful earth makes one retch and want to vomit. Nor is it simply the suffering and destruction that cause physical qualms, but the crushing oppressiveness of human sinfulness and folly, the readiness of human beings to destroy their species and their world rather than turn from their evil ways. Is it not blasphemy to speak in such a context of the love of God? Is there not an insulting glibness in continuing to talk of Christian hope?

Well, despite the almost unbearable incongruity, I still hold that we must speak of the love of God even in the midst of nuclear destruction, but we can do so only at the cost of some further reflection on what is implied by God's creation of free human persons. I want to make a number of overlapping points. God's action in history comes from the divine wrath as well as from divine love, though love is the all-encompassing reality. That action is hidden, not directly manifest, so that an epiphanic vision of God's relation to history, claiming to identify the actions of God is mistaken. Lastly, the apparent triviality of sin hides an enormity which is manifest in its calamitous consequences.

"Autonomy is not a defiance but a grace." That remark of William Lynch in his book, *Christ and Prometheus*,[13] calling for a new image of the secular, states pointedly that God's gift of nature and of grace does not conflict with or hinder human freedom, but is the very gift of that freedom. God's grace is human freedom rendered effective. In other words, God acts in history only in and through human freedom. We must cease to conceive of the divine agency as to any degree replacing human agency or even as working alongside of human agency, complementing it though at a higher level. God is the creative source of human agency, penetrating and transcending it, but God's action in history is mediated through human action. It is not an additional agency operating within the finite order. Its mode of action is to be the perennial, never-ceasing creative source of that finite order. Thus, if the nuclear threat is avoided and the human species changes its social and political behaviour, it will be through the action of human beings themselves. We cannot look for a divine action apart from human agents. The divine action is through those who open themselves in repentance and love to God's gift of their freedom.

That means that human history in the concrete expresses the divine wrath as well as the divine love. Human beings turn away from the offer of their freedom. They fail to love. They are not open to a reality that takes them beyond themselves, but they close themselves upon their own narrow purposes. They sin, and they become a centre of destruction and evil in human history. Like the divine love, the divine wrath is not found apart from human action. It is God as allowing the failure or nothingness of sin, as the absence of a loving response, and then remaining as creative source while human beings work out the destructive consequences of their sin. If human beings refuse to repent of the behaviour that is leading them to nuclear disaster, God will allow them their sin, nor will he suspend his ongoing creative support of the material universe and of human agency to prevent the destruction that behaviour will bring. With God we are dealing with the creative source of this universe as it is, with its evil as well as its good, its terror as well as its beauty. He therefore transcends our categories, our limited concepts of good, of love, and so on.

If the action of God in history is always mediated through human action, the divine action is hidden as well as expressed in human history. There is no direct, unambiguous manifestation of God in history. That is why we speak of the divine wrath as well as of the divine love, of the divine permission of sin and willing of its consequences as well as of the divine gift of grace. We have to renounce an epiphanic vision that claims to identify without ambiguity or question the acts of God.

Even the action of God in Christ is shrouded in ambiguity. I do not mean that we cannot reach the assurance of faith that God was in Christ reconciling the world to himself,[14] but I do mean that the Christian fact in its concrete, historical reality does not bear only one simple, positive interpretation. For example, many Christians like myself want now to say that God was also present elsewhere in history, so that Christian exclusiveness is at best culturally relative, at worst a cultural arrogance. Further, no interpretation of Christ or Christianity is now acceptable that deprives the Jewish religion of its continuing legitimacy. That brings under question much of the history of Christianity from the New Testament onwards. In general, the biblical history of salvation is a symbolic construction, expressing our experience of the reality of the divine love, the ground of our faith and hope. It should not be taken as a simple description of the concrete reality and shape of the historical events it recounts nor should we identify these directly and unambiguously with actions of God. In the biblical period as well as in the late periods, human history hides as well as expresses the nature and purposes of God.

There is, however, an element in biblical teaching, especially in the prophets and in the New Testament, which we have neglected in this modern age and the nuclear threat should bring more sharply to our attention once again, namely, the iniquity of sin. We have trivialized sin, because it is trivial in its appearance, and we have refused the spiritual insight that revealed its enormity. We have dismissed as exaggerated the prophetic denunciations of sin and the saints' bewailing of their own sinfulness, forgetting that, if sin is trifling, the Crucifixion becomes a ridiculous parody of the human condition.

Most sin is trivial in its appearance. I am sure that if we met the leaders, politicians, business men, policy-makers, scientists, technologists who are making the decisions that are driving our societies to destruction, we should judge them to be decent men, struggling to do their best in difficult situations. To the spiritual eye, however, they are in fact, as we ourselves are, embodiments of human pride, arrogance, greed, prejudice, self-centredness, hatred, injustice, vanity, and wilful blindness. The enormity of our failure to love and practise the good is shown by the fact that, rather than embracing the virtues necessary for us to live together in peace, we now are preparing to destroy the human species. We are persisting — perhaps we shall persist to the final blast — in holding that the nuclear threat is merely a social and political problem to be solved by intelligence, instead of acknowledging that it is a state of cumulative sin to be overcome by repentance. It is the sin, not the physical destruction that should make us vomit.

To turn again, in conclusion, to our Christian hope. We cannot elude the problem of evil by simply dissociating God from it. This actual universe with its shadow as well as its glory comes from God. Even if we say he only permits sin and indirectly wills physical evil, the universe as a whole with its sin and suffering was evaluated and chosen by God as its creative source, and the divine evaluation is beyond our apprehension and leaves us perplexed. God cannot be judged in human terms. All the same, evil for the Christian is subordinate to good, so that love has the final word. It is the experience in inward consciousness and in outward action of the reality of that love, of the reality of the kingdom, which is the ground of our Christian hope in the midst of the present darkness. That hope is not easily won. It is found today in agony rather than in ecstasy. Its cost is high. But Christians were never promised an easy salvation, without repentance or a painful transformation. Less than ever in this nuclear age is God's grace cheap.

Notes

1 *Maclean's*, 14 November 1983, p.62.
2 Jonathan Schell, *The Fate of the Earth* (New York: Knopf, 1982).
3 E.P. Thompson, "Notes on Exterminism, The Last Stage of Civilisation," *Our Generation*, 15, No. 1 (1982) pp.5-25. Reprinted from the *New Left Review* #121, May-June 1980.
4 Thompson, p.17.
5 Richard L. Rubenstein, *After Auschwitz: Radical Theology and Contemporary Judaism* (Indianapolis: Bobbs-Merrill, 1966).
6 James M. Gustafson, *Ethics from a Theocentric Perspective: I Theology and Ethics* (Chicago: University of Chicago Press, 1981). See my review in *Canadian Philosophical Reviews/Revue canadienne de comptes rendus en philosophie*, III N. 4 (1982),pp. 173-5.
7 For a discussion of these points, see Stanley M. Hauerwas, "On Surviving Justly: An Ethical Analysis of Nuclear Disarmament," in *Religious Conscience and Nuclear Warfare. 1982 Paine Lectures in Religion*, ed. Jill Raitt (University of Missouri-Columbia).
8.Ronald Green, "Moral Axioms for the Nuclear Age," in *Religious Conscience and Nuclear Warfare. 1982 Paine Lectures in Religion*, ed. Jill Raitt (University of Missouri-Columbia), p. 26.
9 Nicholas Lash, *A Matter of Hope: A Theologian's Reflections on the Thought of Karl Marx* (London: Darton, Longman and Todd, 1981) pp. 271-3.
10 Rom 8:24-5.
11 Lash, pp. 271-3.
12 Rom 5:5.
13 William F. Lynch, *Christ and Prometheus: A New Image of the Secular.* (Notre Dame, Indiana: University of Notre Dame Press, 1970) p. 140.
14 II Cor 5:19